Pop Flies & Line Drives is a "winner," particularly from a human interest standpoint. It was interesting to me to learn things about old friends that I haven't seen for awhile or had lost track of over the years. I found it to be very enjoyable reading.

Mel Parnell
Boston Red Sox 1947 – 1956

If you're into baseball, **Pop Flies & Line Drives** is great reading. Having lost contact with a lot of fellow players over the years, it meant a great deal to us to read about what has happened with them. It was like "old times" again!

George and Billie Spencer
New York Giants 1950-1955
Detroit Tigers 1958, 1960

To Howard—
My locker room neighbor at Dodgertown and a fellow lover of the great game of baseball. May you always hit line drives and never take a called third strike!

POP FLIES
&
LINE DRIVES

Visits With Players From Baseball's "Golden Era"

Best wishes!

by
Jack Heyde

Foreword by: Carl Erskine

Note for Librarians: a cataloguing record for this book that includes Dewey Decimal Classification and US Library of Congress numbers is available from the Library and Archives of Canada. The complete cataloguing record can be obtained from their online database at:
www.collectionscanada.ca/amicus/index-e.html
ISBN 1-4120-3889-8
Printed in Victoria, BC, Canada

TRAFFORD

Offices in Canada, USA, Ireland, UK and Spain
This book was published *on-demand* in cooperation with Trafford Publishing. On-demand publishing is a unique process and service of making a book available for retail sale to the public taking advantage of on-demand manufacturing and Internet marketing. On-demand publishing includes promotions, retail sales, manufacturing, order fulfilment, accounting and collecting royalties on behalf of the author.

Book sales for North America and international:
Trafford Publishing, 6E–2333 Government St.,
Victoria, BC V8T 4P4 CANADA
phone 250 383 6864 (toll-free 1 888 232 4444)
fax 250 383 6804; email to orders@trafford.com

Book sales in Europe:
Trafford Publishing (UK) Ltd., Enterprise House, Wistaston Road Business Centre,
Wistaston Road, Crewe, Cheshire CW2 7RP UNITED KINGDOM
phone 01270 251 396 (local rate 0845 230 9601)
facsimile 01270 254 983; orders.uk@trafford.com

Order online at:
www.trafford.com/robots/04-1697.html

10 9 8 7 6 5 4 3 2

I dedicate this book to all the people that contributed to bringing my knowledge and love of baseball to life and to those who have indulged and supported my lifelong interest in the game, including my hobby of autograph collecting, which has consumed much time and involved considerable travel.

In memory of:

My parents and grandparents, who introduced me to the game and enthusiastically supported my interest and active participation in it throughout my youth. My father, Bill, while working shift work at Cincinnati Gas & Electric Company, sacrificed many hours of his time to coach teams that my brother and I played on. My step-mother, Vera, spent every Saturday morning during baseball season keeping the score and records for the teams we played on. My mother, Peggy, was an ardent fan and never too busy to put on a baseball glove and play "catch" with me when nobody else was available. My grandfather, Irvin Davis, was an outstanding ambidextrous amateur pitcher in his youth and was my most frequent companion at Crosley Field attending Cincinnati Reds games when I was growing up. He also supplied me with Opening Day tickets to Reds games each year. My grandparents, Henry Heyde and Sonoma Davis spent many hours listening to radio broadcasts of Reds games with me when I was growing up.

To:

My wife, Barbara, who has indulged, supported, and, at times, tolerated my baseball passion in many ways. She has sacrificed the time that has been consumed by my several years of coaching youth baseball, as well as many extra nights and weekends that I have spent pursuing my hobby of autograph collecting. She has also yielded the many hours and evenings that I have spent writing this book. Through it all, she has been a constant source of encouragement and support.

My Oakwood High School baseball coach, Marty Armbruster, who contributed greatly to my knowledge and understanding of baseball strategy and tactics, giving me a deeper appreciation for some of the game's nuances and finer points.

The players I have visited, including many not included in this book, who have given unselfishly of their time and experiences and helped resurrect memories of a great time in my life, as well as their own.

ACKNOWLEDGEMENTS

I wish to acknowledge the following individuals for the specific contributions they made to making the publication of this book a reality:

Cyndy Monie, who suggested that I document the highlights of my player visits, with the prospect of someday writing a book about my experiences;

Bruce Abel and Don Clawson, for reading the manuscript and for providing suggestions and encouragement;

Sheila Cockrell, for her outstanding work and attention to detail in editing and proofing;

Carl Erskine, George and Billie Spencer, and Mel Parnell for reviewing the manuscript from the subjects' point of view, and for their encouragement and contribution of testimonials for promotional use;

Bill and Virginia Voiselle, for providing the photo of the 1944 National League All-Star team.

FOREWORD

I just finished reading **Pop Flies & Line Drives: Visits With Players From Baseball's "Golden Era"** and I recommend it to anyone who wants an "up close and personal" acquaintance with some of baseball's real professionals. I was fascinated to read about several players I knew personally, on the field and off.

It's true these are not all Hall of Fame inductees, but every player had some Hall of Fame days, weeks, or years. They were quality major league players, contributing to baseball in the grand era of the 1940s and '50s.

With only eight teams in each league and huge minor league systems, competition for only 25 positions on each team at the top produced a very high quality of play.

I knew these players, mostly as opponents, and I learned a lot about what it was like from their side of the encounters we had. You'll learn a lot too. Read on!

Carl Erskine
Brooklyn Dodgers 1948-1957
Los Angeles Dodgers 1958-1959
17 March 2004

PROLOGUE

It was Labor Day weekend, 1991, and I had little to do at my home in Danville, CA. I had noticed an item in the newspaper about a sports memorabilia show being held at Moscone Center in nearby San Francisco. I decided it might be an interesting way to spend a day. I had been active in sports throughout my life, particularly baseball. I had played on organized teams from the age of 8, when my dad enrolled me on one of Cincinnati's many Knot Hole teams, through high school and college. One of the greatest thrills that I experienced as a young ballplayer was playing a game in Crosley Field, the Reds home park, when I was in high school. I later coached and played on an excellent fast pitch softball team, which played in the championship game of the 1965 U.S. Navy Atlantic Fleet tournament, during my stint as a naval aviator. More recently, I had coached youth baseball teams, including high school teams, from 1980 – 1993.

BIRTH OF A PASSION

Although my interest in professional baseball had been considerably dampened by league expansion, free agency, and the player and umpire strikes during the 1980s, I still had a warm place in my heart for the game and particularly for the players who had played when I was growing up in the late 1940s and throughout the '50s. My first baseball memory is of the 1947 season. That was the year Jackie Robinson broke baseball's color barrier. Ewell Blackwell won 16 consecutive games and pitched a no-hitter for the Reds against the Boston Braves. In his next start, "Blackie" came within 2 outs of duplicating Johnny Vander Meer's 1938 feat of pitching consecutive no-hitters when he surrendered a one out, ninth inning single to the Dodgers' Eddie Stanky. In the World Series that year, the Yankees' Bill Bevens lost a no-hitter and the game when Dodgers' pinch-hitter "Cookie" Lavagetto doubled off the right field wall with 2 out in the ninth inning of game 4 at Ebbets Field and, in game 6, Dodgers' outfielder Al Gionfriddo made a spectacular catch to rob Joe DiMaggio of a potential game tying home run in Yankee Stadium. I was only 8 years old, but I listened to both of those games on the radio and, from that year on, I was hooked on baseball.

CINCINNATI

Although I lived with my mother and went to school in Dayton, I spent considerable time in Cincinnati, visiting my father and my grandparents during my childhood. Cincinnati was a great place to grow up, if you liked baseball. Everyone loved the Reds, although they were, at best, a mediocre team in the '40s and early '50s. But it had not been long since they had won the National League pennant in 1939 and defeated the Detroit Tigers in the 1940 World Series. My mother was an ardent Reds fan and had attended the sixth game of the 1940 series. She loved to talk about having seen Bucky Walters hit a home run to help win his own game, in game 6 of that series, and about her favorite player, Ival Goodman, the right-fielder. Cincinnati also had Waite Hoyt, a former Yankees pitcher and baseball Hall of Famer, broadcasting Reds games on the radio. Hoyt was a fascinatingly entertaining and knowledgeable broadcaster, who would tell stories about Babe Ruth and Hoyt's other Yankee teammates during delays in the game's action. I remember being glued to the broadcasts of the games. On one side of town, in Cheviot, I would listen to the games with my grandfather and my uncle in the basement, which was the coolest part of the house in the summer, before air-conditioning became prominent and affordable. On the other side of town, in Mt. Lookout, where my other grandparents lived, I would listen to the games with my grandmother. We would sit outside on a glider, under the awning on the back porch, and feed peanuts to the squirrels, with an electric fan blowing to help stay comfortable. My grandfather would join us for night games, which were rare in those days, or for weekend games when he wasn't playing golf. In the '50s, when night games became more prevalent and my grandparents had purchased a television, we would sit in the living room, listening to the radio broadcast of the Reds baseball game, while watching professional wrestling on TV, with the sound turned off, as radio was still the primary medium for baseball and few games were televised in Cincinnati.

Radio broadcasts of the Reds games were an important part of my developing love for the game, because they stimulated my imagination and kept me engaged in the action, by forcing me to visualize what was happening. In those days, the Reds broadcasters did not travel with the team. Away games were reconstructed by the broadcasters from the local broadcast studios, where they received details of the game's progress by a code transmitted via Western Union telegraph from the home team's stadium. As a result, there were often lulls in the broadcast when you could hear the telegraph ticker in the background, as the information was being received over the wire. There would be a lull and suddenly you could hear the ticker start. It sounded like an expert typing on an old-fashioned typewriter and you knew that something important was happening in the game. Good radio broadcasters had to be creative in order to create the illusion that they were broadcasting from the actual site of the game, rather than from the studio. Broadcasters like Hoyt, with his baseball playing experience, were particularly effective at filling in the "dead time" between ticker transmissions with imaginary information about what might be taking place, given the game's situation or circumstance. Broadcasts of the Reds games were sponsored by the Burger Brewing Company, a Cincinnati brewery, and Hoyt always referred to a home run as "a Burger blast" or he would say, "He hit one into 'Burgerville'."

Opening Day of the baseball season has always been a major event in Cincinnati. The Reds always open the season at home, an honor bestowed in recognition of their being the first established professional baseball team, and I attended every Opening Day game from the time I was 10 years old until I left for college. Being a good student, I was always allowed a holiday from school for Opening Day and frequently took a classmate with me to attend the game. April weather is unpredictable and I remember watching "openers" in every imaginable type of weather, including snow, but I don't recall an Opening Day in Cincinnati being postponed in all the years I attended.

Organized youth baseball was an integral part of Cincinnati culture. The city's love for the Reds flowed naturally into the youth culture. The Knot Hole program had hundreds of teams (classified by age) throughout the city, providing organized baseball opportunities to kids from 8 to 16 years old. The teams and leagues were sponsored by local merchants and coached by teachers or parents who were knowledgeable about baseball. Games were played on Saturday mornings and, when the Reds were playing at home, Knot Hole players were admitted to Saturday afternoon games free of charge. At the end of the Knot Hole season, champions from the many leagues throughout the city competed for the overall city championship in each age classification. The ultimate city champions were honored at an awards banquet, which always included an address by a prominent professional baseball figure. I was fortunate enough to play on a championship team in 1950, when Larry Goetz, a senior National League umpire, was the speaker.

Cincinnati also had very active American Legion and senior amateur baseball programs. In the late '40s and throughout the 50's, Cincinnati's Bentley Post was a perennial contender for the national American Legion baseball crown, winning the title several times under the tutelage of an old schoolteacher named Joe Hawk. Joe was sort of short and had a high squeaky voice, but he knew baseball and had access to some of the best baseball talent on Cincinnati's west side, from Western Hills and Elder high schools. Dick Drott, Don Zimmer, Gordy Massa, the Nixon twins (Russ and Roy), Jim Brosnan, Art Mahaffey, Eddie Brinkman, and Pete Rose are some of the players who played on Bentley Post teams.

When not involved in formal team practices or games, my brother and I spent the day with other kids, playing baseball type games like "one-o-cat," "fungo," or "hot box," that could be played with 3-6 players. We would ride our bikes to the park after breakfast, play until noon, go home for lunch, return to the park for an afternoon session, and be back home in time to clean up and set the table for dinner. After washing and drying the dinner dishes, we would ride our bikes to the recreation center to watch night softball games, always being sure to be home at the designated time, so that we didn't lose our privileges. In bad weather, we spent the day organizing our baseball card collections or "flipping" baseball cards (a game similar to shooting marbles) with friends, in an attempt to augment our collection. From my growing up years in Cincinnati, baseball has been in my blood.

RENAISSANCE

So, it was a combination of curiosity and a yearning for some nostalgia that led me into San Francisco that Labor Day, 1991. The scene in Moscone Center surprised me. It seemed mind-boggling. I didn't realize what a big business sports memorabilia had become. The hall was filled with fans and collectors visiting booths offering every conceivable item of memorabilia (trading cards, programs, ticket stubs, pins, pennants, bats, balls, photographs, replica uniforms, old posters, scorecards, magazines, audio and video tapes of memorable sporting events). Every major sport was represented, but the majority of the merchandise was related to baseball. After browsing the hall for a couple of hours, I engaged Bill Henderson, a baseball card dealer from Wisconsin, in conversation about old baseball cards. The collection I had accumulated as a kid, which included cards issued from 1948-1953, had been thrown away by my parents when I left for college (a common story told by many childhood collectors). After talking with Bill and looking through his inventory, I decided to start a collection of the 1954 Topps baseball cards. The set was attractive artistically, small in size (250 cards), affordable, and picked up where I had left off collecting as a youth. I purchased a "starter" set of 75-80 cards from Bill and began my quest to complete the set, which I accomplished in 2-3 years.

In the course of completing my card set, I attended other memorabilia shows and became interested in items that had been autographed by players that I had followed and seen play when I was growing up. I already had an autographed item that may still be the most valuable item I own. It is a game-used baseball autographed by Eppa Rixey and Ethan Allen. (Rixey is a Hall of Famer who was the winningest left-handed pitcher in baseball history until Warren Spahn broke his record. Ethan Allen was an outfielder and subsequently became President George Bush's baseball coach at Yale.) The ball was given to me by my grandfather, who caught it at a Reds game in 1926. He took it to the dugout, where Rixey and Allen autographed it for him.

UP CLOSE AND PERSONAL

The first autographed item that I purchased was a "limited edition" bat autographed by members of the 1957 Milwaukee Braves world championship team who attended the team's 35th reunion, held in Milwaukee in 1992. Only 57 of these bats were issued. Two members of the team, Wes Covington and "Nippy" Jones, had not attended the reunion and, therefore, had not autographed the bat. My new quest became to locate the two ballplayers and add their autographs to the bat. I quickly determined that "Nippy" Jones lived in nearby Sacramento. That was the good news. The bad news was that Wes Covington had left the country to avoid tax obligations and was not likely to return. He was living in Edmonton, Canada. I managed to contact "Nippy" Jones, who, although not in good health, agreed to let me visit him at his home in Sacramento, where he added his autograph to the bat. It was this visit that set me on my course of visiting former players in their homes and adding to my autograph collection. "Nippy" and his wife were so gracious and accommodating when I visited their home that I decided it would be fun to visit other former players whom I remember watching play when I was growing up. As for Wes Covington, I'm still trying to catch up with him.

With the Milwaukee Braves bat as a starter, I purchased some special, team specific bats from the Cooperstown Bat Company, some generic bats, and a supply of official National and American League baseballs to have autographed and expand my collection. My job at the time involved occasional travel throughout the United States, which gave me an opportunity to identify, contact, and visit many former ballplayers in the evenings or on weekends. I also attended occasional sports collectors' shows when they included a significant number of autograph guests. These events, however, usually did not offer the opportunity for meaningful conversation with the players. So, individual player visits became the focus of my efforts, because they afforded an opportunity for dialogue.

In seeking out individual players, my approach was to write a letter explaining my collection, stating when I was coming to town, and requesting a meeting to obtain that player's autograph for my collection. When I arrived in a city, I would telephone the player, following up the letter I had sent. An overwhelming number of the players contacted in this way were agreeable to meeting with me, either at some convenient public location (coffee shop, restaurant, shopping center, hotel) or, most frequently, at their home. Visits in players' homes were the most productive, interesting, and enjoyable and it was not uncommon to be offered snacks, a drink, or even invited to stay for a meal. For players whose phone numbers were not listed, I would stop by their home, apologize for the unannounced visit by explaining that I was unable to contact them by phone, and refer to the letter that I had previously sent. In such cases, I do not recall a player's refusing to visit with me if he was at home. After a visit, I recorded the highlights of our conversation in a journal, which became the basis for this book, and always followed-up with a "thank you" letter to the player and his wife, if she was present during my visit.

My visits with most of the players usually resulted in conversations about baseball and their playing experiences; however, in some cases, players shared with me intimate stories of personal and family experiences unrelated to baseball. Frank Thomas, Bob Purkey, Cal Hogue, and Pete Castiglione (all former Pittsburgh Pirates) are a few that come to mind. Some players I visited were not in good health. Ron Kline was recovering from surgery on his foot, for problems related to diabetes. Bill Voiselle had suffered multiple strokes. Bob Dillinger was recovering from his third hip replacement. Some players passed away shortly after my visit. "Nippy" Jones, Allie Reynolds, "Frenchy" Bordagaray, and Paul Giel are among them. One thing about all of the players mentioned in this book is constant. They were all very accessible, gracious, hospitable, and humble people, who were willing and happy to visit and share memories with a fan of the game, when baseball truly was "America's pastime."

SHARING THE EXPERIENCES

The idea to document my conversations and experiences with the players was suggested to me a few years after I had begun my visits. Cyndy Monie, the wife of our church pastor, was a dinner guest in our home one evening. She took particular interest in both my collection and the activity associated with it and asked if I maintained a journal of my visits. When I replied that I did not, she persuasively suggested that I begin doing so, in order that I could share some of my experiences with family and friends. "You might even want to write a book about your hobby someday," she pointed out.

Well Cyndy, here it is! I hope you enjoy reading it as much as I have enjoyed the experiences themselves.

BOB BUHL
St. Louis, MO
April, 1994

I meet Bob at a baseball card signing show in St. Louis, where Johnny VanderMeer is also a guest and is drawing most of the attention, giving Bob more time than usual to visit with the patrons. He is tall, trim, and appears to be in excellent condition. His trademark dark, thick eyebrows make him easily recognized by anyone familiar with the Milwaukee Braves pitching staff in the 1950s. Pitching as the number 3 starter behind Warren Spahn and Lew Burdette, Buhl made a reputation for himself by his complete mastery of the Brooklyn Dodgers, the perennial National League power in those years.

"Bob, you made a virtual career out of beating the Dodgers. What was it that made you so effective against them?" I ask.

He smiles broadly, pauses for a moment, and explains, "Well, when I was being scouted, Brooklyn was the first team to show some serious interest in me, but they decided not to offer me a contract. So, I guess when I finally made it to the big leagues I had a certain determination about showing them they had made a mistake by not signing me. I got a definite thrill out of beating them and always had a very sharp focus when I pitched against them. Of course, it also helped that they had a predominantly right-hand hitting lineup, what with my being a right-handed pitcher and all."

Knowing that Bob had experienced disastrous results in his two World Series starts against the Yankees in 1957, I venture onto dangerous grounds by saying, "You didn't have quite the same success against the Yankees in the '57 Series. What do you think happened there?"

Still smiling, he chuckles and replies, "That's one of those experiences you'd just as soon forget. I'm not sure why, but I just didn't have anything against them. 1957 was a great pitching year for me…may have been my best…but you'd never know it by those two starts. Control was a real problem for me in those two games."

Others are now waiting to meet Bob, so I thank him for his time and sharing with me and wish him the best of luck.

Bob Buhl died February 16, 2001.

ALLIE REYNOLDS
Oklahoma City, OK
August, 1994

I call Allie from Don and Roberta Carter's house. They are close personal friends from 1969-71, when I lived in Oklahoma, and we are visiting them for the weekend. Allie answers the phone and I explain the purpose of my call and ask if he would sign a couple of items if I stop by his house. He quickly agrees, gives me directions, and adds, "Now, when you get here, don't leave if I don't answer the door right away. I don't get around too well anymore and it may take me a bit to get there."

When I arrive at Allie's house, the front door is open and Bill Mangum, Allie's attorney, is standing at the screen door. I have met Bill previously through a mutual friend, Doug Hamilton, who is an attorney in Oklahoma City and shares my interest in collecting baseball memorabilia. I renew acquaintances with Bill as he directs me into the kitchen, where Allie is seated at a table. I am aware, from conversations with Doug, that Allie is not in good health. He has many ailments, which include cancer, lung disease, and diabetes. Even seated, Allie is a bear of a figure. He has a barrel chest, broad shoulders, huge arms, and his hand seems to completely engulf my own as he greets me with a handshake and a rather tired smile. “Don’t mind if I don’t get up,” Allie says, “it’s just easier if I stay seated.”

“No problem. I’m just glad to have the opportunity to meet you,” I tell him.

Allie signs several bats and a couple of balls for me. His hand is somewhat shaky.

“These bats are tough to sign anymore,” he says.

“You’re doing great,” I encourage. “Allie, tell me how you used to pitch to Ted Williams.”

He grins. “Most of the time I just walked him!”

We talk a little about the World Series match-ups with the Brooklyn Dodgers in the late 40s and early 50s that Reynolds so frequently dominated, but, realizing that my visit is tiring Allie, I thank him for seeing me and wish him the best.

As I leave the kitchen, I come face to face with a large portrait of Allie hanging on the wall of the entry foyer. It is a head and shoulders painting of Allie in a Yankee pinstripe uniform, wearing a full Indian chief head dress. The caption reads “Super Chief.” It is an impressive piece and it is the last I will see of Allie Reynolds.

Allie Reynolds passed away December 26, 1994, four months after my visit.

TOM HENRICH **"Old Reliable"**
Anaheim, CA
September, 1994

My meeting with Tom takes place at a card signing show at the Anaheim Convention Center. I wait until the line of patrons getting autographs diminishes so that I can talk to him without holding up other people. When he finishes signing the items I have, I ask him a couple of questions.

"Tommy, you played with both DiMaggio and Mantle. Which of them do you think was the better hitter?"

He responds promptly, "Oh, Joe was clearly the better hitter. Mickey probably had more power, but Joe was a better hitter. You see, with Joe, you might get him out with a certain pitch one time, but you didn't get him out with the same pitch twice. That wasn't the case with Mantle. You could get him out with the same pitch time and again. Of course, you had to be able to control the pitch and, eventually Mickey would make an adjustment, but Joe adjusted immediately. You just didn't fool him twice!"

I change the subject to pitching. "The Yankees had really great pitching in the late 1940s and '50s. Raschi, Reynolds, Lopat. If you had one game you had to win, which of those guys would you want on the mound for you?"

"Well, those guys were all pretty good, but that little fella' right over there was about as good as they get," he says, motioning to Whitey Ford, who is sitting at a table across the room. "I think I'd probably take my chances with him."

FRANK CROSETTI **"The Crow"**
Stockton, CA
July, 1996

It's late afternoon on a hot summer day when I arrive at the small, single-story frame house in a quiet, older residential area in Stockton. Frank has given me directions to his home and greets me at the door with a friendly smile and a handshake. He is wiry, spry, and alert. He moves about smoothly and with a purpose that belies his 86 years. Time has been good to Frank Crosetti.

"What can I do for you?" he asks. "It sounds like you're quite a baseball man. Let's go sit down in the kitchen and talk about it."

Looking over the two Yankees bats that I have given him to sign he comments, "Gee, you've got some great stuff here. These are some real ballplayers. Tommy Henrich…a real 'gamer.' Allie Reynolds…they don't get much better. Gene Woodling…another great one. Where do you want me to sign this?"

"Anywhere you'd like," I reply.

After Frank completes signing the bats and a couple of balls for me, I show him a team photo of the 1951 Yankees team that I have brought. Having identified all but 8 or so of the players in the photo, I ask Frank if he can help me with the others. He quickly identifies 3 or 4, but is having difficulty with the remainder.

Studying the figures intently, Frank comments, "Let's see, this guy was a pitcher…had a funny nickname…hmm. And this fellow was a catcher…can't recall his name right now. Tell you what. Give me a few days and I'll figure it out and let you know."

I can't imagine that Frank will give the matter further thought and, happy to have the help he has given me, try to dismiss it. "Oh, it's no big deal. Don't worry about it. Thanks for your help with the others."

Handing the photo back to me, he gets up out of his chair and says, "Come on in the other room and I'll show a few things of mine." He leads me to a room that serves as a sort of office or display room. There are a modest number of baseball photos on the wall and he comments casually about some of them. He shows me a couple of his World Series rings and then takes a small case from off a bookcase and opens it. "Look at this. I'll bet you haven't seen many of these. It's a World Series watch. Before they started the tradition of giving out World Series rings, the Yankees management used to give us a new watch when we won a World Series."

Frank shows me some autographed baseballs and other items and then we return to the kitchen, where I gather my stuff and prepare to leave. While walking to the front door with me, Frank says, "I'll get back to you on that photo. I have your address from the letter you sent me."

"Oh, don't worry about it. It's not that important. I just appreciate the time you gave me. Thanks a lot for everything," I say, as we shake hands and part.

Approximately 10 days after my visit with Frank Crosetti, I received a note in the mail at my home in Dallas. Handwritten on a note card with a red border and a baseball embossed in the upper left-hand corner is the following message: "J.W. - The player end of row is Stubby Overmire. The player next to Brideweser is catcher Gus Niarhos. Player near Mantle is pitcher Bobby Hogue. Player on top row I think is pitcher Fred Sanford. Hope this does it for you. Still hot today. P.S. Forgot to give you this picture." (signed) Cro

Enclosed with the note was a photo of a young Frank Crosetti in his Yankees uniform, inscribed: "Best Wishes to J.W. Heyde" (signed) Frank Crosetti.

Frank Crosetti died February 11, 2002.

KEN RAFFENSBERGER
York, PA
March, 1998

Ken is at the door of his trailer park home just outside York when I arrive. He has anticipated my arrival, having given me directions to his home only a few minutes earlier on the phone. He is portly and virtually bald. He welcomes me with a handshake and a smile and invites me into the house.

We sit at his dining room table, where he autographs a Reds bat, a NL bat, and a ball for me. "What do you remember most about your career as a ballplayer?" I ask.

He muses, "Well, I was not a great pitcher by any account. I had to rely on control and a variety of pitches. My best pitch was a knuckleball. Probably the greatest compliment of my pitching was the fact that Stan Musial always said that he hated to bat against me. To have a hitter of Musial's quality say he hated hitting against me is quite a tribute. I'm pretty proud of that."

"What manager did you most like playing for?" I ask.

"I think Bucky Walters was my favorite manager. He was a former pitcher and he understood pitchers and how to treat them. I remember a game I pitched in Wrigley Field for the

Reds against the Cubs. I pitched a 2-hit shutout and after the game I asked Bucky if I could have a couple of hours added to my curfew. I had a friend who was a cop in Chicago and he liked to take the visiting ballplayers out to some local clubs when we were in town. Bucky gave me the curfew extension and handed me a $20 bill, which was worth a lot more in those days than it is now, and said 'Go have yourself a good time tonight, you earned it.' That's the kind of guy Bucky was. He made you want to play well for him," Ken says.

Ken comments about how much he liked Ray Mueller as a catcher and asks if I know whether Mueller is still alive. I tell him Mueller died several years ago and Ken expresses his disappointment at the news. As I get ready to leave, Ken leaves the room for a minute and returns with a photo of himself, which he autographs and hands to me. "Here, this is the picture I send to people who write to me for an autograph," he says.

Ken Raffensberger died on November 10, 2002.

DUANE PILLETTE
San Jose, CA
July, 1998

Living in a trailer park south of San Jose, which he managed for several years, Duane is still trying to reorder his life following the death of his wife in April, after a lengthy battle with cancer. He is tall, soft-spoken, quite pleasant and accommodating as we sit in his living room and he tells me about the changes he is planning to make to his home. The furniture is old, the atmosphere is quite shaded, almost dark, and seems a bit bleak. There is a certain disorder to everything. A woman's presence is clearly missing, in both the house and in Duane's life.

Duane tells me some "Yogi" stories from his days as a Yankee. We talk a little about Ned Garver, Duane's former St. Louis Browns teammate, whom I had met at a Cincinnati Reds Old-Timers' golf outing a year earlier. Then Duane tells me about the last game the St. Louis Browns played in Sportsman's Park, a game in which he pitched.

"Bill Veeck, the Browns owner at the time, was a real 'skinflint.' For all the publicity he generated in his lifetime, Veeck was a real tightwad when it came to spending money. When we played the last game in St. Louis, Veeck had taken his supply of baseballs right down to the end. By the end of the seventh inning, we had run out of game balls! We had to play the last two innings of that game using the balls that had been used in batting practice that day! It was the damnedest thing you've ever seen. I'll never forget it!"

As I am leaving, Duane shows me his wife's car, which he says he will have to sell soon, as it has not been driven since she passed away.

BOB USHER
San Jose, CA
July, 1998

I arrive at the Ushers' home, a modest house in an old residential area on the north side of San Jose, and find a note taped to the front door: "Jack - We're in the back yard, please come on back."

Having called earlier to make sure I would not be interrupting their mealtime, I am surprised to see Mrs. Usher putting utensils on the patio table, and Bob starting to take barbequed chicken off the charcoal grill as I enter the back yard. "Oh hello, we're just having dinner. Would you care to join us?"

Politely declining, I ask them to please proceed with their meal, which they do, while we talk about Bob's playing days in Cincinnati. There are repeated requests to have me join in the meal, which I decline. Taking a break from his meal, Bob autographs the Cincinnati Reds bat and, while doing so, takes time to look carefully at some of the signatures already on the bat and offers comments about several of the players he remembers. He chuckles as he recalls a collision at home plate that he had with Andy Seminick, when Seminick played for the Phillies. He tries again to persuade me to join in the meal. "We've got plenty of chicken and this corn is really good. Are you sure you won't have some? How about something to drink?"

Having another appointment to keep, I again decline, but delay my departure to allow Bob to talk a little more about his playing days in Cincinnati and with the Cleveland Indians. He is clearly enjoying recalling highlights of his career in baseball.

LLOYD GEARHART
Xenia, OH
November, 1998

Lloyd Gearhart is the first professional baseball player I ever met. I was only 8 years old in 1947 when Gearhart, then concluding his only year as a member of the New York Giants, spoke to a group of youngsters at a Methodist Church in Centerville, Ohio, where my family was living at the time.

Arriving at his small home outside Xenia, I am greeted by Lloyd with a smiling look of recognition. Lloyd remembers our previous meetings at the charity golf outings sponsored by the Heart Association of Cincinnati, in conjunction with annual Cincinnati Reds "old timers" reunions in 1996 and

'97. I have brought with me a New York Giants bat that I did not have at the time of previous meetings and want to add Lloyd's autograph to it.

Our meeting begins outside on the porch on a cool and windy day. Lloyd scans the bat and asks me about Jack Lohrke and Bill Rigney, whose signatures he notices. After giving him an update on the two, Lloyd insists that I come in the house and meet his wife. Penny Gearhart takes leave of her apple pie making to sit down in the living room and join us in talking about baseball and various other matters, including the loss of their son, Marty, at age 40, to a recurrent melanoma and the paralyzing injuries sustained by another son, Steve, in an auto accident some years earlier. We discover we have some common acquaintances in the Dayton area and share several stories about them. Lloyd says he needs to make a quick trip to Kinko's at a nearby mall and asks if I would drive him over so we can continue our conversation.

Lloyd recalls his 1947 season with the Giants, the only year he spent in the major leagues, and how the team dealt with the arrival of Jackie Robinson. "We had some good players on our team," Lloyd begins. "Mel Ott was the manager and we had guys like Johnny Mize, Walker Cooper, Larry Jansen, Sid Gordon, Willard Marshall, and Bill Rigney. Cooper had been around awhile and didn't particularly like the idea of Robinson's playing, so, whenever Jackie came to bat, Coop would say, 'Better get ready, nigger; because you're goin' down!' Robinson retaliated by just wearing out our pitchers and, finally, Mel Ott told Cooper, 'Keep your mouth shut! The guy is killing us!'"

When we return to the house, Penny offers me a piece of her "fresh out of the oven" apple pie and Lloyd shows me a ring that was given to all Giants players on the '47 team, commemorating the record 221 home runs the team hit that year. Lloyd likes to point out that he and Johnny Mize accounted for 57 of those 221, although Mize hit 51 and Gearhart only 6!

"There's a strange story about this ring," he begins. "I used to keep this ring on top of the dresser in our bedroom whenever I wasn't wearing it. One day it was missing and I had a pretty good notion that one of my son's friends might have taken it, but I wasn't sure. When it didn't turn up after a few days, I reported it to the local police, who, of course, know me pretty well. Well, that ring went missing for a couple of years and then one day I got a phone call from one of the fellows in the sheriff's office. He said that someone had found the ring in the glove compartment of a used car that they had purchased and called to see if anyone had reported it missing! We have no idea how it wound up there, but I sure was happy to get it back. It's a one-of-a-kind item, you know."

As I prepare to leave, Lloyd goes into another room and returns with copies of several autographed photographs from his playing days with the Giants, as well as one of Mel Ott. Handing them to me, he says, "Here, take these along with you. You can include them with your collection."

Lloyd Gearhart died December 2, 2001.

HARRY DANNING **"The Horse"**
Valparaiso, IN
November, 1998

At 87 years of age, Harry Danning is in remarkably good shape and health when I visit him near Valparaiso, IN, where he lives with his daughter and son-in-law. Harry has his own quarters, an apartment type arrangement with its own entrance, on the second floor of his daughter's home. He still has his own car and drives whenever he feels like getting out for a while. He says he has some problems with his knees and really doesn't care much for getting old ("Aging sure is a humbling experience."), but moves around quite well, although he uses a cane to help get up and down the steps to his apartment. His apartment is heavily decorated with pictures from his long and active life as a ballplayer, an employee of Metropolitan Life, a husband, and parent. He makes a point of showing me a picture of himself and his wife (a quite attractive woman who passed away 20 years ago), which was taken in 1940.

I explain to Harry that I first became aware of him while reading about Willard Hershberger's suicide in 1940, during the Cincinnati Reds' pursuit of the National League pennant. Hershberger, the Reds backup catcher to Ernie Lombardi, was pressed into regular service when Lombardi went down with a season ending injury. Danning recounted the story himself. It was late in the season and the Reds were struggling to maintain their shrinking lead in the pennant race, when they played the final game of a series with the Giants in New York. Cincinnati, with Bucky Walters pitching, held a 4-1 lead late in the game when Danning hit a home run that was the key blow in a Giants rally that ultimately resulted in a Giants victory. The next day, in Boston, Hershberger failed to show up at the ballpark for a game with the Braves and was subsequently found dead in his hotel room. He had slashed his wrists with a razor blade. It was speculated that Hershberger blamed himself for the pitch that Danning hit for the homer that ultimately resulted in the Reds loss to New York, and that his ensuing despondency over the event precipitated his suicide. Danning's comment about the event is clearly heartfelt: "If that was the reason Hersh took his life and I had known what was going to happen, I would have rather struck out!"

Danning is part of a unique piece of baseball trivia. He is one of three players to be ejected from a game by three different umpires as the result of a single play. The Giants were playing in Cincinnati when Harry Craft, a Reds outfielder, hit a ball over the left field wall, which Danning claims everyone clearly saw as a foul ball. Everyone, that is, except the umpires, who ruled it fair and a home run! Danning and Joe Moore, the Giants left fielder, both had good looks at the play and immediately took violent issue with the umpires; Danning with Lee Ballanfant, who was behind the plate, and Moore with the third base umpire, who Harry was unable to identify. Meanwhile, Billy Jurges, the Giants shortstop, took up the battle with the first base umpire, George Magerkurth. Danning was ejected by Ballanfant, Moore was ejected by the third base umpire, and Jurges was ejected by Magerkurth. (Joe Moore later provided me with another perspective on this particular play, which he claimed played a pivotal role in the pennant race that year.)

Danning played for Giants managers Bill Terry and Mel Ott. While he had been a team mate of Ott's for several years and felt a personal kinship with him, Danning felt that Terry was the better manager and easier to play for. "When they made Melvin manager, someone told him he had to be 'tough' on the players. He underwent quite a change in his personality and, in the process, lost touch with many of his players. He was a wonderful person and knew the game well, but managing was not his strength."

I ask Harry what it was like to play in the Polo Grounds. He feels the stadium "took away" more than it "gave away." While the short distances down the left and right field lines were attractive targets for dead pull hitters, the rest of the outfield was a cavernous graveyard for many power hitters. "It was 420 feet to the wall in the power alleys in left-center and right-center field and 465 feet to center. Teams learned to give up the left and right field lines and 'bunch' their outfielders toward center, making it extremely difficult to hit a ball between the outfielders for extra bases." While the park was admittedly unusual in its layout, Danning feels it was a good park to play in.

Asked about the Giants storied rivalry with the Brooklyn Dodgers, Danning recalls an incident that he claims symbolized the nature of the rivalry. Playing in Ebbets Field, Danning recalls a game in which Ed Head of the Dodgers had a no-hitter going into the late innings when Danning broke up Head's bid by singling. When he reached first base he was pelted by three lemons, which had been thrown from the stands. "Those people in Brooklyn were the wildest and loudest fans in the league. You never knew what to expect when you played over there!"

Harry declines my offer to take him to lunch, but says he'd be glad to join me another time, if I'm back in the area.

DICK BOKELMANN
Arlington Heights, IL
November, 1998

Bokelmann expresses pleasant surprise when I call to try to make an appointment with him. He says that while he would be happy to sign, he was not a very prominent player. When he looks over the St. Louis Cardinals bat that I ask him to sign, he comments, "Gee, I really don't belong on a bat with all of these guys!"

Humble and reserved, Dick talks about his one partial season with the Cardinals. A pitcher, he was called up from Rochester, and pitched in relief the night he joined the Cardinals. "Marty Marion was the manager and he wanted me to know that he had confidence in me, so he used me right away. Marty was a great manager in that respect. He knew that self confidence was a key to succeeding in the big leagues, and he did everything he could to help build that confidence." Dick expressed great admiration for Marion, Stan Musial, Enos Slaughter, Red Schoendienst, and his other teammates from 1952.

Dick regrets that he did not save any reminders of his partial season in the majors. He is occasionally active with a group of former major leaguers living in Chicago and says that Johnny Klippstein has done a good job of keeping some of the old players together. He has fond memories of Gerry Staley, who he says is a "real class person," and encouraged me to look up Staley, who he says is living in Oregon. Dick thanked me for coming by and gave me an autographed reprint of his 1953 Topps baseball card.

JIM BROSNAN
Morton Grove, IL
November, 1998

Having both grown up in Cincinnati, it wasn't hard to make conversation with Jim, a graduate of Elder High School and a former member of the Bentley Post American Legion baseball team. The Bentley team dominated Cincinnati and Ohio amateur baseball until new rules were put into place in the late 1950s to restrict Bentley's access to some of the area's best high school players. (Bentley Post still holds the record for most American Legion National Championships won by a single post team, and it was this type of success that precipitated the rules changes that were implemented by the American Legion baseball program to curtail Bentley's dominance of the national tournament.) Brosnan recalled losing his position as Bentley's shortstop to a younger player named Don Zimmer, from rival Western Hills High School.

Jim is quite proud of the contribution he feels that he and Bill Henry made to Cincinnati's 1961 National League championship team. "The bullpen was a great part of our team's strength. With Henry as the left-handed reliever and me as the right-hander, we had a very strong bullpen." He recalled Gabe Paul's taking strong exception to some of the material included in Brosnan's book, particularly an exchange that took place between him and Ernie Broglio after the two had been traded for one another by the Cubs and Cardinals.

We have some further conversation about local Cincinnati baseball people and Jim mentions that he had just been advised that he was going to be inducted into the Cincinnati Sports Hall of Fame next spring. Although he is about to undergo replacement of both knees, he hopes to be able to attend the induction ceremony.

"FRENCHY" BORDAGARAY
Ventura, CA
December, 1998

It's Sunday morning when I call Ventura from LA to see if "Frenchy" will allow me to stop by to add his autograph to my Dodgers bats. His wife, Victoria, answers the phone and, when I explain the purpose of my call, says quite directly, "Oh, he'd love to do that. When can you come up?" She gives me directions to the house and says to call if I have any trouble finding it. It is a surprisingly accommodating response.

At 88, "Frenchy" Bordagaray is a joy to be around. Although struggling with Alzheimer's symptoms and strongly dependent upon his delightful and attentive wife, "Frenchy" loves recalling his athletic achievements. Somewhat surprisingly, he prefers talking about his achievements as a track and football star at Fresno State, rather than his days as a professional baseball player with the Dodgers and two World Series teams (the '39 Cincinnati Reds and the '41

World Champion New York Yankees). Bordagaray wants me to know that he was an All-America Football Player at Fresno State in 1930, and Victoria wastes little time breaking out an All-America Football Team membership card awarded to "Frenchy," containing the names of the authorizing committee members on the back of the card (Amos Alonzo Stagg, Knute Rockne, "Pop" Warner, among others). "Frenchy" also maintains that he still holds the Fresno State record in the 100 yard dash (a claim that seems unlikely, but may be worth checking).

Victoria invites me to look through "Frenchy"s scrapbook, which consists of 2 stacks of photocopies of full page newspaper clippings dated from 1928-1942. She also shows me his lifetime pass to Major League Baseball games, which is a silver on copper piece that she says she polishes periodically with toothpaste. ("Silver polish is too expensive and the toothpaste doesn't contain abrasives," she says). As I browse through the newspaper clippings, "Frenchy," who is seated across the table from me, reads the column headings upside down and adds his commentary to many of the articles and pictures. "I was the fastest player of my day. Nobody could outrun me," he comments.

Periodically, he loses his thought and Victoria quickly comes to his assistance. At other times, she corrects him, particularly about dates and peoples' names. She tells him how to hold the pen so that his signature will be more steady and helps him locate a suitable place on the bats for his signature. "Frenchy" asks me to remember him to Pete Coscarart, a former teamate, whom he knows I am planning to see the next day.

As I am about to leave, "Frenchy" has an accident with his bowels and Victoria must go to help him get cleaned up. "It's so hard to see him get old after being married for 57 years," she says. I leave feeling privileged to have met and visited with "Frenchy" and Victoria, a very gracious and hospitable couple.

"Frenchy" Bordagaray passed away April 13, 2000.

CLIFF DAPPER
Fallbrook, CA
December, 1998

Finding Cliff Dapper's house in Fallbrook would be a challenge in the full light of day. Trying to find it at night is a true odyssey. Despite having a detailed map and written directions obtained from the Mapquest website, along with Cliff's own directions, I spend approximately 30 minutes and have to ask further directions from 4 different people within 2 miles of his house! When I finally find the electronic gate to the area in which he lives, I wait another few minutes to gain access, as his phone is busy.

Since my "wanderings" have made me late and it is now very close to dinner time, my visit with Cliff is brief and pretty much limited to having him sign my Dodgers bats. Cliff, who played in only eight games as a backup catcher with the 1941 Brooklyn Dodgers, is dressed in denim bib overalls when he greets me at the door. As he signs the bats at a desk next to the kitchen, where his wife is preparing dinner, he asks if I have visited "Duke" Snider, who he says lives just over the hill. I tell him I have visited with "Duke" on several occasions, but never at his home. Not wanting to delay the Dappers' dinner, I thank them both and quickly take my leave. Cliff offers an alternative route for my return to Del Mar, but I choose to use the way I now know to be easiest for me.

PETE COSCARART
Escondido, CA
December, 1998

My Mapquest map and directions to Pete Coscarart's home in Escondido work fine. None of the problems like I had finding Cliff Dapper. When I arrive, Pete has gone out to run a quick errand and I am invited in by Pete's wife, who is carrying some bags from her car into the house. She sets her bags down on the kitchen counter and immediately shows me the pictures of her children and grandchildren, which line the top of a bookcase that runs the length of the family room adjoining the kitchen. She asks me if I would like a sandwich, or something to drink, perhaps a Coca-Cola. I decline and ask her if she has any more bags in the car that I might bring into the house for her. She says she has everything and tells me to just sit down and make myself at home until Pete returns, which she is sure will be shortly. Within minutes, Pete walks in through the garage.

Pete asks me some questions about my hobby as he looks over the many autographs on my Dodgers bats. He notes Mickey Owens' signature and asks when I met Mickey and how he was doing. He recalls the famous "third strike passed ball" that eluded Owens in the ninth inning of a 1941 World Series game that allowed Tommy Henrich to reach first base and the New York Yankees to rally and win a game that should have belonged to Brooklyn. "I was playing second base when that happened and I can recall that play as though it were yesterday. I'm sure that (Hugh) Casey threw a spitter. He often threw it in a tight situation. That ball broke so sharply, Mickey had no chance to catch it, but I thought he would retrieve it in time to throw Henrich out at first base. I was running over to back up Dolph Camilli on the throw when I saw the ball roll into the dugout. Next thing you knew, the game was over. Casey cried like a baby in the clubhouse after the game." Pete's wife is quick to mention that Hugh Casey was a wonderful person and always fun to be around.

Knowing that I have been to see "Frenchy" Bordagaray, Pete asks me how he is doing and then we talk for a few minutes about Dolph Camilli, Pete's teammate on the Dodgers. I comment about how fit Camilli seemed when I saw him at a baseball show in Long Beach in 1996 and mention how surprised I was to hear that he had passed away earlier this year. Camilli, I believe, was 90 years old at the time I met him and appeared to be in his 60s (trim, sharp, alert, steady, energetic). He had told me that he played golf almost every day and that regular activity was the secret to "staying young." Pete's wife says that Camilli was fine until he was in an accident late last year. Apparently, one of his injuries led to an infection that the doctors were unable to control and Camilli's system eventually succumbed to the infection. Pete mentions that he too plays golf regularly (at least once or twice a week) and shows me a golf bag that he was given for playing in a recent Roger Craig Benefit Golf Outing. He says I should come back sometime when I have time to play golf with him. He walks me out to my car when I am leaving and says how much he has enjoyed meeting and talking to me.

Pete Coscarart died July 24, 2002.

BOB DILLINGER
Canyon Country, CA
December, 1998

Bob is "puttering around" in his garage when I arrive on a weekend morning. As he sees me getting out of the car, he inquires, "Are you the fella' with the bats?" I respond that I am and, taking the appropriate bats from the car trunk, follow Bob through the garage and into the house. Bob walks with an obvious stiffness in his legs and, when I ask him about it, he replies, "I'm just coming off my third hip replacement. Its been about two months now." The most recent replacement is a "re-do" of a hip replacement done 11 years earlier on Bob's right hip. Increasing problems with arthritis resulted in the need to "replace the replacement" and Bob seems to need to stay on the move, as he constantly shifts his position and frequently gets up to walk around during my brief visit.

"Do you have much pain with it?" I ask.

"No pain, just kinda' stiff," he says.

We sit at the breakfast room table while Bob autographs the items I have brought in and we talk baseball. I ask him if he sees any of the other players of his day.

"No, I don't have much to do with baseball anymore, although I do try to attend the annual meetings of the local Association of Baseball Players," he answers. "There are more former minor league players than major leaguers, but Sparky Anderson is quite active with the group. But that Dodgers guy who claims he bleeds Dodgers blue can't even find time to respond to our invitations." He is speaking of Tommy Lasorda and it is immediately apparent that Bob has little respect or use for Lasorda.

Bob seems justified when I tell him that, having had my own brief experience with Lasorda, I can understand his feelings.

Our conversation somehow rolls around to Ferris Fain. Fain, it seems, was not only a former teammate of Dillinger's, but a close personal friend and comrade during Bob's years in the military. Bob's wife joins the conversation. "When Bob and Ferris were in army camp together, Ferris got to missing his wife so much that he decided to go AWOL to visit her. Bob answered roll call for Ferris for several days while he was gone and, somehow, they never did figure it out. When Ferris returned, nobody had missed him!"

Bob also talks respectfully of Connie Mack, his general manager and field manager during Bob's years with the Philadelphia A's and says that he is planning to go back to Philadelphia for the next A's Historical Society meeting. As I prepare to leave, Mrs. Dillinger asks if I would like to have a photograph of Bob with Connie Mack. Bob goes to another room and returns with an 8"X10" photo and a copy of one of his baseball cards, which he autographs for me before I leave.

CARL ERSKINE
Anderson, IN
November, 1998

Carl and I agreed to meet at the Star Bank, of which he has been president for many years. When I arrive, his secretary ushers me into Carl's office, where he greets me with a smile and a handshake. The office is decorated modestly and tastefully with a few photos and baseballs, memorabilia of his playing days as a pitcher with the "Boys of Summer," the Brooklyn Dodgers of the 50s. When I called to make the appointment, I had been the first to notify Carl of the passing of Charlie Neal, a former teammate, who had died recently in Texas, so Carl is anxious to talk about Neal.

"I'll never forget one particular situation that involved Charlie Neal. Cincinnati had a pitcher named Raul Sanchez, who was used mostly as a 'mop-up' pitcher when a game was already lost. He had a reputation, at least with the Dodger players, as being a guy who would always knock somebody down late in a game. One day in Cincinnati, Sanchez drilled Jim Gilliam in the ribs with a fastball. Gilliam was a pretty quiet guy and he didn't react at the time, but he made up his mind that he would get even someday. Well, a few weeks later the Reds came into Brooklyn for a series and, sure enough, Sanchez comes in late in one of the games and up comes Gilliam. So Gilliam drags a perfect bunt down the first base line and, when Sanchez comes over to field the ball, Gilliam pounces on him and proceeds to start pounding him with his fists. Of course, both benches empty and begin pouring toward the site of the fight. One of the Reds players coming out of the third base dugout was Don Hoak, a real 'roughneck.' Hoak had his eyes locked on Gilliam and never saw Charlie Neal, who had come out of our dugout and had his eyes locked on Hoak. Charlie let go with a right hand punch that landed square on Hoak's jaw and sent him about five steps backward where he fell backwards over the pitcher's mound. He never knew what hit him. Several players from both teams were ejected and suspended and the next time the Dodgers went to Cincinnati, Warren Giles, the National League president, called a hearing in his office in the Carew Tower with Hoak and Neal. Ted Kluszewski and I, as the team representatives, were also required to attend. Mr. Giles lectured the two regarding expected future conduct and concluded the meeting by saying, 'Now I want the two of you to shake hands and forget what happened.' Hoak looked at Charlie Neal, then at Mr. Giles and said, 'I'll shake his hand, but I'll never forget what happened!'"

I follow up with a question about Kluszewski, whom I remember well as a monstrous physical presence on the field. "What sort of a guy was Kluszewski?"

"Ted was a wonderful guy. He had those huge arms and we hated pitching against him because he hit really hard line drives and a lot of them were right up the middle, through the pitcher's mound. He had a very unusual swing in that he didn't use a lot of wrist. He hit a little bit stiff-armed, but you didn't have much time to react because he hit the ball so hard. He hit Bubba Church in the face with a line drive that almost killed Church, and certainly shortened his career. Another time he hit a ball back through the middle against Johnny Podres and Podres hit the deck to avoid being hit. The ball goes into center field and when Duke (Snider) returned the ball to the infield, Podres is still flat on the ground, not moving. He hadn't been hit but, in his haste to get out of the way of the ball, he had twisted his knee. He was out of action for a couple of weeks."

Carl continues, "The other thing I remember about Ted was his wife. She was a little bit of a thing and Ted, of course was a really big guy. Ted used to have a few of us over to his house for dinner when we went to Cincinnati, and I'll never forget how he 'jumped through hoops' when his wife told him to do something. It was really pretty cute."

"What was it like playing in Ebbets Field?" I ask.

"Ebbets Field was quite a unique ballpark. There were a lot of very unusual things about it. For instance, a section of the rightfield wall was concrete. It went up about 15 or 20 feet high, but the bottom half had an angle to it, so that a ball hitting the lower half of the wall might carom in any direction. Carl Furillo learned how to play balls off that wall like a magician, but other outfielders had nightmares with it."

"Then there was the scoreboard that was above the wall in right-center field. It was an old-fashioned, hand operated scoreboard, where someone walked around inside the scoreboard and hung the numbers on the scoreboard from the inside. Right next to the scoreboard was a big Schaefer Beer sign and the "H" and "E" in the name Schaefer were outlined with neon tube lights to signal whether a play had been scored as a "hit" or an "error." Both the scoreboard and the sign were located inside the park, so that a ball hitting either was not a home run, but a ball in play. One day I was pitching against the Giants and Hank Thompson hit a ball that hit the Schaefer Beer sign and somehow got stuck between the sign and the neon tube in the "E." While Thompson is running around the bases, Furillo is standing there banging on the wall, trying to dislodge the ball so that he can make a play. The ball stayed stuck and Thompson circles the bases and is awarded an inside-the-park home run. Then we had to stop the game while the grounds crew put up a ladder and retrieved the ball from the sign so that we could continue the game," Carl chuckles.

He continues, "Our bullpen in Ebbets Field was down the right field line, in foul territory, right against the right field wall. We always had a chair right up against the wall and right next to the foul line. Whoever sat in that chair always had a white towel. He HAD to have a white towel. Whenever a fly ball was hit toward the right field wall with runners on base and less than 2 out, the players in the bullpen could usually tell, better than the baserunners or coaches, whether the ball could be caught or was going to hit the wall. If the ball was going to hit the wall, the player with the towel would stand up and start waving the towel, so that the runners knew that they could run without fear of being 'doubled up'."

"What sort of guy was Jackie Robinson?" I pose.

"Jackie was just a wonderful person," Carl responds. "I'll never forget in 1948 I was with Ft. Worth and we played a pre-season exhibition game against the big club. I pitched and had a pretty good day and, after the game, Jackie came up to me and said, 'You keep pitching like that and you'll be up with us in no time.' Later that year the Dodgers called me up and, when I walked into the clubhouse the first day, Jackie was the first person to come over, put his arm around me and say, 'See, I told you you'd be here pretty soon.'"

I thank Carl for his time and the stories. Before I leave, he suggests that I consider attending a Dodgers Fantasy Camp week in Vero Beach, Florida sometime and wishes me a safe trip.

CAL HOGUE
Dayton, OH
November, 1998

Cal Hogue lives only a couple of miles from the home where I grew up in Dayton, Ohio and he is quite willing to let me stop by for a visit. As it turns out, Cal and his wife are close friends of Virginia and Marty Armbruster (my high school baseball and football coach), who live right around the corner. We talk for awhile about Marty's health and some local community matters. When I ask him about his family, Cal tells me about his daughter, who, at age 33, was hit and killed by a young hit-and-run driver.

"She had just left a restaurant and was walking across the street to get in her car when she was hit by a young girl, who left the next morning for a vacation in Florida. When she was finally apprehended, she was fined $1000 and spent 30 days in jail," Cal concludes, shaking his head in quiet resignation.

"How do you think the game of baseball has changed?" I ask.

"Oh, today it's all about money," Cal says. "A few years ago, Ron Nishwitz and I were asked to join several of the current Cincinnati Reds players at an autograph signing show. When the time that we had all agreed to sign was up, there were still several people in line waiting to get autographs. Ron and I stayed the extra 15-30 minutes to accommodate everyone, but the Reds players weren't about to stay for a minute longer than the time they were being paid for. They simply got up and left."

After signing my bats, Cal asks me how I got started with the hobby. Seeing a sincere interest on his part, I go to the car and return with a couple of my heavily autographed bats to show him. He smiles and makes some short comments about some of the names that he sees as he looks them over, notably, Jack Lohrke, a former roommate. He wishes me luck and tells me to stop by again sometime when I'm back in town.

DAVE WILLIAMS
Farmers Branch, TX
January, 1999

Sue Williams, Dave's wife, is recovering from the flu, so Dave meets me in the parking lot outside their condominium in Farmers Branch, a suburb of Dallas. It's a cold day and Dave is wearing a red turtleneck under a royal blue Fila warm-up suit. He's also wearing a Texas Rangers baseball cap. "You must be Jack. I'm Dave Williams," he says as I step out of the car. "I'd like to ask you in, but my Sue's still got a bit of the bug and you don't want any part of it. She's had it since we returned from Las Vegas a week or so ago."

Our conversation is mostly about baseball and golf. Seeing some of the names on my Giants bat seems to ignite memories and Dave offers some stories, particularly about Lloyd Gearhart, who Dave thinks of as sort of a "character."

"Lloyd was sort of a wild baserunner. Some baserunners are considered 'daring,' but Lloyd was just 'wild.' One day he was on first base and took off when he thought a hit ball was going to fall safely. When the ball was caught in the outfield, Lloyd was about halfway between second and third and Kiki Cuyler, the third base coach, was waving frantically for Lloyd to return to first. When Gearhart finally realized the situation, he turned and cut diagonally across the pitcher's mound to return to first. Of course he was called out but, when asked why he had done it, Lloyd's answer was: 'It was the only way I could beat the throw!'"

Dave also had some stories about Johnny Mize. "Mize used to drive me crazy. Every day he would talk forever about the dog races the night before and how he bet them and the details of every damn race. It got so bad that I would go to the park an hour early just so I wouldn't have to dress with him and have to listen to all the stories about the dog races." Another Mize story involved Jack Lohrke and was not particularly flattering of Mize. "In '47, when the Giants set the single season team home run record with 221, Lohrke, I believe, hit the last home run – the one that set the record. Lohrke didn't hit a lot of home runs and Mize, of course, hit 51 that year. Lohrke wanted his picture taken with Mize, but Mize refused and Lohrke never did get his picture taken with Mize."

Another Lohrke story involves the famous 1951 final playoff game against the Dodgers, the "Shot Heard Round The World" game. "At the start of the bottom of the ninth inning, when the Dodgers took the field leading 4-1, Robinson went to the mound and shook Newcombe's hand. It was a terribly arrogant and inflaming thing to do, but I'll never forget Lohrke's saying to me, 'Well, you piss on the fire and I'll call the dogs,' meaning that he thought the game was over." The Giants, of course, wound up winning the game when Bobby Thomson homered with two on to win 5-4.

Dave tells me about a day a few years ago when his oldest grandson, 17 years old at the time, was visiting and telling Dave about how fast he could run. Dave challenged him to a footrace of about 30 yards in the parking lot and beat him. "My wife couldn't understand why I didn't let him beat me. I told her 'He'll beat me soon enough and then I'll never beat him again. I'll be damned if I'm just going to let him beat me.'"

Dave continues the story: "The next day I'm taking my annual physical at the doctor's office and they put me on the treadmill for a stress test. About a minute and a half into the test, the doctor yells out, 'Get him off of there! Take his clothes and put him in the hospital, right now!' When I asked him what was wrong and told him I had just run a race with my 17 year old grandson the day before, he said, 'You're lucky to be alive.' The next day I had a four-way bypass operation."

Like most former ballplayers, Dave enjoys playing golf and is active with the Major League Baseball Players Alumni Association golf outings, particularly in Texas. Dave says his backswing is limited by chronic back problems, but he still enjoys playing.

I tell Dave to wish Sue a quick recovery from the flu as I get ready to leave.

BILL WERLE
San Mateo, CA
August, 1998

Bill Werle is a gracious and accommodating host, particularly for a short notice visit. He is happy to talk with me and to show me his extensive collection of memorabilia, which fills most of an expansive recreation room in the basement of his San Mateo home. Although a bit profane, he displays a friendly and engaging personality.

Bill wastes little time in getting to the matter of autographing the bats that I have asked him to sign. While he is signing, he talks about his ongoing activities in professional baseball, as a scout for the Cleveland Indians. He explains that he scouts both American and National League teams when they play in Oakland or San Francisco. It keeps him quite busy and the fact that the game has changed substantially since his own playing days does not seem to bother him. He invites me downstairs to his basement recreation room to see his own collection.

The four walls of the room are covered with press photographs, including a great many actual game action photos, virtually all of which are autographed by the subjects in the photos, including umpires. It is an incredibly extensive and unique collection. Bill explains, "I had a friend who was an AP (Associated Press) photographer. He regularly gave me prints of the wire photos used in those days and I made it a point to get the pictures autographed, whenever I could." In one corner of the room is a bar that Bill has built himself. The face of the bar is made of baseball bats that have been sawed in half lengthwise and placed vertically to form the face of the bar. The bar stools are also Bill's handiwork, the legs being baseball bats, with bases used as the seats. The top of the bar counter is covered with more photos, which are protected by a glass or plexiglas counter top. More bats are displayed on the wall behind the bar.

"This room was almost ruined a few weeks ago," Bill comments. "My wife and I were supposed to go to an out of town wedding for the weekend. At the last minute, I decided to stay home. On Saturday morning, I woke up and heard water running. It was too early for the sprinklers to be on, so I got up and started looking for where the water was running. I finally wound up coming downstairs and found about three inches of water on the floor and water gushing out of a pipe in the ceiling of the laundry room. If I hadn't been home to discover the problem, no telling how much water would have wound up in this room. There's no place for it to go!"

I comment about how unique and valuable this collection, particularly the autographed action photos, must be. When Bill merely shrugs his shoulders, I suggest that he have someone appraise his collection and to talk with his insurance carrier about insuring it. "Oh, I guess it might be worth something to some people, but to me it's just a reminder of my ballplaying days."

WALLY WESTLAKE
Sacramento, CA
August, 1998

As I pull up in front of the Westlake house, Wally walks from the garage, where he has been "puttering," directly to my car and greets me with a handshake. He is wearing blue Levi bib overalls, has large hands, and a firm grip. He has a pleasant smile and demeanor, and looks as though he has worked hard all of his life. As I begin to take the items from the car that I want him to sign, I ask how his wife is doing. (We had re-scheduled our meeting from Tuesday to Wednesday due to Mrs. Westlake's need to complete a physical therapy treatment following a recent stroke.) "She's doing fine. She has these mini-stokes every once in awhile, but so far nothing too serious." We chat about our families for a few minutes at the curb and he invites me to come into the house. We sit at the table in the breakfast room and the conversation quickly turns to baseball.

"I owe my career in baseball to Casey Stengel. When I came out of the war (WWII), I was 24 years old, which was a little late to be trying to start a career in professional baseball. A friend of mine and I managed to talk our way into a tryout in spring training with the old Oakland team in the Pacific Coast League. In those days, the Pacific Coast League was a first class league, with lots of good ballplayers, many of whom went on to play in the majors. Stengel was the manager at Oakland and he did everything he could to discourage us. He assigned both of us to the "B" squad, which meant that we worked out on a separate field, with none of the amenities that the "A" squad enjoyed. We had rocks on the field, no drinking fountain, and worked out with used balls. It was miserable. Every once in awhile we would sneak into the "A" squad batting practice – just so we could hit some decent balls – and he would always chase us back to the "B" squad field. We were working our asses off trying to get him to notice us, but really felt we didn't have much of a chance, since he spent all of his time with the "A" squad. The day before we broke camp to go north, Stengel called us into his office and said, 'I know you guys have been working hard and I'm taking you both with me on the main roster. I'll pay you $400 a month and travel expenses.' I was thrilled to death, but told him I'd have to have $450 or I was going home! And you know what? He gave it to me! The thing about Stengel was: he made me work on my game at all times and taught me how rewarding it could be to work hard. He really knew the basics of the game, positioning, hitting the cutoff man, bunting, and alert and intelligent baserunning. Lots of people think of him as a crackpot, but the man really knew his baseball."

We talk for a while about some of the other ballplayers in the area that I hope to visit, Ferris Fain, Ed Fitzgerald, Marv Grissom, and then I thank him for his time and the autographs. He walks me back out to the car and somehow, before I leave, we wind up in a conversation about our children and the differences in raising children in the 90s and what we remember of our own upbringing. We agree that we are glad we have no more children to raise! Wally invites me to stop and visit again anytime I'm in the area.

MAX LANIER
Dunnellon, FL
January, 1999

Scheduling a meeting with Max is difficult, not due to a lack of willingness on his part, but because of uncontrollable circumstances that limit the time he is available. Max had called me in Dallas when he received my letter requesting a meeting, to tell me that, although he had suffered 2 heart attacks and a stroke and his wife was undergoing daily radiation treatments for breast cancer, he would be glad to sign anything I wanted, provided I could come by on a Saturday or Sunday! With my weekend sales meeting schedule, limited opportunities are available, but, fortunately, we find time to get together.

When I call to set-up our meeting, Max tells me that his wife is in the hospital, but he will be home if I can get there around 4:00PM. I suggest that perhaps it would be better if we wait until another time. "No, I have no problem if you can get here around 4 o'clock."

It's already 3:15 and I estimate the drive at an hour, but I pack my stuff and head for the Lanier's, arriving at 4:30. Max sees me pull in the driveway, opens the door, and waves hello to me with a smile. "I did the best I could Max, but the traffic held me up a little."

"Don't worry about it; come on in," he says as he shakes my hand. Entering the living room, I notice two original oil portraits hanging on a wall opposite the sofa that Max has invited me to sit on. One is of Max in his Cardinals uniform and the other is a somewhat smaller one of his son, Hal, in a Houston Astros uniform. Once seated, I ask about Mrs. Lanier.

"She's having a pretty tough time of it. Had about six months of chemotherapy after removal of a breast and now she's taking radiation. She's having some problems with her heart from the radiation and they're trying to get everything to work together. She's in good spirits though and is still eating well." I tell him a little about my own experience with chemotherapy and radiation and wish Mrs. Lanier the best with her treatments.

As he looks over the bats before signing, Max comments about some of the players whose autographs he sees. "Davey Williams. He was playing second base behind me in the easiest game I ever pitched. We were playing Cincinnati in the Polo Grounds. The score was tied in the top of the ninth and Ted Kluszewski was coming to bat for Cincinnati with a man on first and one out. I was a starting pitcher most of the time, but Durocher called me out of the bullpen to pitch to Kluszewski. I threw one pitch and he hit into a double play. In the bottom of the ninth, Whitey Lockman hit a home run to win the game for us. I was the winning pitcher and had only thrown one pitch!"

"Hank Sauer. He beat me one day when he was with the Cubs. 14 innings. I pitched all 14 innings and was tied 1-1 in the 14th at Chicago. Stan Musial and Marty Marion each made an error in the 14th, which was most unusual for either one of them. Anyway, Sauer never should have come to the plate, but he beat me with a homer after those two errors."

I ask Max about his decision to jump to the Mexican League in 1945.

"Well, I had pitched for the Cardinals when they won the pennant in '42, '43,' and '44. I pitched in the World Series each of those years and in 1944 I had won 17 games and we had won the World Series. In 1945, as a reward for my contributions, I was offered a $500 a year raise. I signed my contract with the Cardinals, but when the Mexicans offered me a lot more money to play down there, I decided to take it. Actually, the Cardinals disappointed me many times. It seemed like they were always backing down on their commitments. I finally began requiring them to include their commitments in my written contract."

Max shows me a newspaper clipping from his playing days, highlighting how he had beaten the Brooklyn Dodgers 11 straight times as a Cardinals pitcher before they finally broke the string. I mention Larry Jaster's similar success against the Dodgers in the late 60s. We talk about some players he has seen recently at get-togethers nearby. Ted Williams. Virgil Trucks. Tommy Lasorda. Stan Musial. Monte Irvin. I mention that I would like to reach Irvin, but his phone number is unlisted. "Oh, I have it right here. Give him a call. He's a very nice guy."

As I thank him and prepare to leave, Max leaves the room for a minute and returns with 2 color photos of himself in his Cardinals uniform. He signs each of them with a personal inscription, hands them to me and says, "You know, I feel like we've known each other for a long time."

HERSCHELL FREEMAN **"Buster" or "Hersh"**
Orlando, FL
January, 1999

"Hersh" is sitting on the steps of the front porch of his modest home, located not far from the Orlando airport. He welcomes me with a handshake and a smile, without getting up, as his wife comes to the door to ask if I had any problems with her directions to the house.

"No problem at all. It was a 'piece of cake'," I reply.

When I tell Herschell I remember watching him pitch in Cincinnati, where I grew up, he comments, "Well, it's nice to talk with someone who actually saw me pitch. Most people who ask for my autograph tell me their father saw me pitch. I really enjoyed playing in Cincinnati for 'Birdie' (Tebbetts). He was a great manager, because he knew how to chew you out and pat you on the back at the same time. He made you want to play better for him."

"How did you like playing in Boston and Cincinnati?" I ask.

Hersch replies, "I never liked playing in Boston (for the Red Sox). There was always sort of a clique in Boston. If you were part of the 'in' group, it was fine, but if you weren't, you were left pretty much alone. In Cincinnati, there were no cliques and the Reds fan club was always active and supportive of the entire team, even though we didn't have a real good club in those days."

As Herschell prepares to sign my Reds bat, he looks at the autographs already on the bat. Spotting Brooks Lawrence's autograph, he chuckles and says, "One year Brooks started the season by winning the first 13 games he pitched. In those 13 wins, I had 11 saves. 'Birdie' started saying, 'Pitching today will be Brooks Lawrence and Herschell Freeman.' It made Brooksie madder than hell."

As he finishes signing my items, Herschell comments, "You know, people send me cards and stuff in the mail to sign. Sometimes they enclose a check for $10 or so and I always write across the front of the check, 'I do not take money for my autograph' and send it back to them. The only thing I won't do is sign a big stack of cards for someone, because I know they are probably going to be sold. It seems like everything today is about money. And you know what? It's ruined baseball. Steinbrenner and that guy from the A's (Charlie Finley) are the ones who started it. I remember in

1957 I was the second highest paid player on the Reds club. I was making $22,500 and Kluszewski was making $50,000. Today, you've got players making a half million dollars, sitting on the bench, and they can't even play baseball!"

LARRY JASTER
W. Palm Beach, FL
January, 1999

If it can ever be said that a pitcher made a career out of beating one team, it can be said of Larry Jaster. Although his career was not a lengthy one (68 total decisions), he left an indelible mark in the record books with his pitching performances against one of the better teams of his day, the Los Angeles Dodgers. Throughout 1965 and into 1966, Larry Jaster completely dominated the Dodgers, shutting them out 5 consecutive times. It wasn't until the 7th inning in what would have become the 6th consecutive game that the Dodgers finally scored a run against Jaster. The main reason I wanted to meet Larry was because I vividly remembered the accomplishment from having listened to St. Louis Cardinals radio broadcasts in Memphis, where I was living at the time. I wanted to know what, if anything, had contributed to Jaster's accomplishment.

Larry and I agree to meet at Applebee's for lunch. He tells me he will be wearing an orange shirt and black Nike warm-up pants. When I arrive I have no trouble locating him in a booth near the windows. He is drinking a cup of coffee and gets up to greet me with a handshake. He is a big, quiet looking, quiet speaking man. Knowing I have been visiting other ballplayers in the state, he asks if my trip and efforts to get autographs has been a success. His interest seems genuine and I give him a quick synopsis of my visits over the past 2 ½ days. He tells me he is still actively involved in baseball with the Baltimore Orioles organization. He is divorced, with grown children, and has been living with his girlfriend in West Palm Beach for the past 13 years. He seems particularly proud of one of his sons, who is in his third year of medical school at Dartmouth.

We order lunch and I get right to the point of my interest. "Larry, tell me about the unusual success you had pitching against the Dodgers. What was it that made you so successful against that particular team?"

A smile creeps slowly across his face as he begins. "Well, I don't really know. I guess it was a combination of things. The Dodgers then didn't have a lot of power. They depended on speed and I really worked at keeping their speed off the bases. I didn't walk many. And of course Dodger Stadium and Busch Stadium were both pretty big ball parks, which was helpful to a fly ball pitcher like I was. It was a strange thing. Once it got started, it just sort of 'fed' off itself. It seemed like the harder they tried to 'get at' me, the more difficulty they had. I think the only other pitcher to shut out one team 5 times in a single season was Grover Cleveland Alexander, and his were not consecutive. I never pitched against Koufax, but I was matched against everyone else; Drysdale, Sutton, Osteen, and Singer. Sometime after the streak came to an end, I went back over the box scores and discovered that through the entire span of shutout innings I had given up only 24 hits…all singles!"

I have to ask, "Was there any sort of 'baiting' or 'trash talk' going on throughout that streak?"

"No, not really. I wasn't about to say anything. You know, let sleeping dogs lie. And they were so frustrated, they just wanted to beat me. You know, my record in the major leagues was 35 wins and 33 losses. Of my 35 wins, 11 were against the Dodgers!"

We talk a little more about baseball and some of the players Larry likes. He claims a close friendship with Dal Maxvill and Joe Horner, who died in a mysterious farming accident in 1998. "Joe was ploughing a field, where he used to like to hunt, for a friend. Nobody knows what happened, but they found him crushed under one of the wheels of the tractor. He had had a lot of health problems, heart, high blood sugar, a bunch of stuff. Nobody knows whether he fell off the tractor, got off himself, or what."

We wrap up our meeting with some talk about the NBA "lockout," sports salaries in general, and ice hockey (a sport Larry enjoys following now that the Florida Panthers have added Pavel Bure to their team). We walk to my car, where Larry signs the items I have for him and then gives me directions for the best route back to the Florida Turnpike.

TOM SAFFELL
Sarasota, FL
January, 1999

A widower, Tom Saffell lives in a very nice second floor condominium overlooking the water of Sarasota Bay, in a heavily treed, gated residential complex. He is wearing slacks and a T-shirt and seems remarkably fit and active as he invites me in. On the wall is an oil painting of Tom in his Pirates uniform in his left-handed batting stance. He offers me a seat and asks what I would like him to sign. He looks over the signatures on the Forbes Field bat and offers a comment or two about a couple of the names he sees. "I'd like to show you some of my own collection, but first I need to help my secretary back out to her car. She's recently had a quadruple bypass operation and insisted on coming over today to see if there is anything that needs to be done." He leaves the room.

I wonder what it is that Tom does that requires a full-time secretary. A few minutes later, he re-enters the room, assisting a very elderly woman, who is supported on the other side by a younger woman. The three of them are shuffling toward me. “Annie, this is Mister Heyde. He brought some baseball items for me to sign. Jack, this is Annie, my secretary, and her daughter.” We exchange greetings and some small talk and then Tom asks me to wait for him while he helps her down the steps.

When he returns, he is shaking his head. “She really wants to come back to work, but I’m not going to let her. It’s just too much to have her going up and down those steps. I know she’s going to be very disappointed. She’s been with me ever since I took over the job as administrator for the Florida Coast League.” It turns out that the FCL is composed of 3 divisions and Tom handles the administration (scheduling, etc.) for the entire league. It’s a full-time job, year around.
He takes me to one of the bedrooms, which serves as his office. Among the photos on the wall is one of Tom in a flight suit, standing on the wing of a Wildcat fighter. Next to it is a tarnished set of U.S. Air Force pilot wings mounted on red felt in a frame. He tells me he flew several combat missions in Europe during WWII. “Never shot down, but I took a few hits.” He opens a closet door and shows me about 25-30 baseball bats. Among them are many black World Series Commemorative bats. “I have every World Series Commemorative bat that has been issued since 1979. The signatures, of course, are replicas, but it’s still quite a collection.”

He walks me to the door as I prepare to leave and asks me to say “hello” to Pete Castiglione, whom he knows I will be seeing the following day. “Pete was over here for an Old-Timers game a couple of years ago. He can still hit the ball. He had two or three hits that day. Tell him I said ‘hi’.”

PETE CASTIGLIONE
Pompano Beach, FL
January, 1999

Pete and I had 3 or 4 telephone conversations before our meeting, mostly trying to work out the timing for my visit. When I call to let him know I am only a few minutes from the house and would be there shortly, he asks if I need directions. "No thanks," I reply, "I know right where you are and I'll show you something interesting when I get there."

From his living room, Pete sees me pull into the driveway and walks out the front door to greet me. He is trim and clearly in great physical shape. I show him the map to his home that I obtained from the Mapquest website on the internet. "It's really nice, but it's also sort of frightening, if you're someone who treasures privacy," I say. As we enter the house, Pete asks me if I mind if he shows it to his wife and I tell him he can keep it if he wants.

"Honey, come look at this," Pete calls to his wife, who immediately emerges from the other end of their single story home. She is an attractive and athletic looking woman and is dressed in shorts, as though ready to play golf. "Honey, this is Mister Heyde… and this is my wife, Joan," Pete says, as he hands her the computer map showing their name, address, phone number, and a detailed map to their home. She smiles and asks me to sit down, as she looks at the map. She comments that one of her children had shown her something similar recently and we talk for a few minutes about the wonders and the risks that are a part of life with the computer and the internet.

Knowing that Pete is in his mid-seventies, I comment about how fit he and Joan look and ask what they do to stay in such great shape.

"As you can probably guess, Joan is a golfer. She plays several times a week. I still play a lot of tennis," he says, gesturing toward several trophies displayed on the shelf of a bookcase. "I can't play singles anymore, but I get my doubles in every day or two down at the city courts. I still play some local tournaments and this year I'll be in the 75s and older! I can't find the time for golf. I leave that to Joan."

Somehow, while Pete is signing the bats and ball that I give him, the conversation turns to travel and Joan tells me that she is leaving in mid-February on a 16 day trip to China. "Pete's not a traveler, but I love to travel, so I'm going with some of my friends." I tell them about my own love for travel and that my wife, Barbara, like Pete, does not quite share my obsession. I tell them about some of my memories of our trip to China in 1985 and note, from the itinerary that Joan has shown me, that she will be staying in the same hotel that my wife and I visited in Xian. I suggest that she take a few food staples with her, for snacks, as the food in China became quite monotonous for us and a simple jar of peanut butter and a box of crackers was a luxury well worth having.

As Joan prepares to leave for the grocery, Pete asks if I would like a Coke or something to drink. As he goes into the kitchen to get me a glass of water, I look at the family photos that are displayed in the living room. A large color portrait of three girls and a boy, all attractive young adults, hangs on the wall beside the front door. "You certainly have an attractive family, Pete," I comment.

"Yes, we're very proud of them," Pete says, handing me a glass of ice water. "The girl in the middle and our granddaughter were killed in an automobile accident last summer. We're still not able to talk much about it. C'mon back to my room and let me show you what I still have from my playing days."

A short walk down the hall brings us to a bedroom that has been converted into an office, much like his former teammate, Tom Saffell, has. One wall is heavily covered with pictures of Pete, mostly in his Pirates uniform. There are action photos and photos of Pete with various celebrities. "That's me tagging Stan Musial out. There I am with Bing Crosby, who was one of the Pirates owners back in those days. That's Janet Leigh when she was making a movie with us during spring training. There I'm leaning into the box seats to catch a foul pop." I compliment his display and tell him about Bill Werle's unique photo display in the basement of his San Mateo home. (Werle was a teammate of Pete's in Pittsburgh.)

Pete turns to the desk and I see the letter I had written him several weeks earlier requesting to visit. "See, there's your letter. I even marked on it the date I called to tell you to come on by. Would you like to have a picture to take with you?"

Pete takes two sepia toned photos from a stack in the drawer of his desk, autographs both, and adds a personal inscription to one of them before handing them both to me.

Knowing that Pete has been generous with his time and needing to get back on the road for my meeting with Larry Jaster in West Palm Beach, I thank him for his time and hospitality and tell him to thank Joan, as well, and wish her the best on her trip to China.

DAVE FERRISS **"Boo"**
Cleveland, MS
February, 1999

The drive from Memphis to Cleveland down highway 61 brings back memories from the late 60s, when I periodically drove the same route making sales calls on architects and contractors from my base in Memphis. If anything has changed in the intervening 30 years, other than the presence of casinos along parts of the banks of the Mississippi River, it is merely that the area seems even more desolate and abandoned. There is little evidence of life anywhere to be seen. The small towns of Tunica, Mound Bayou, Shelby, and others seem virtual "ghost towns." In Mound Bayou, an early black settlement, a moderate sized hospital sits abandoned, in an advanced state of decay, with windows boarded up. Hardly a person is to seen as I drive through these towns at mid-morning in the middle of the week. Even Clarksdale, a reasonable size town by Mississippi standards, appears to have degenerated and lost most of the life and quaint appeal that I recall.

Following "Boo's" suggestion, I stop at the Hampton Inn in Cleveland and call his house to get directions. His wife, Miriam, answers and tells me that "Boo" is expecting me but has gone to run a quick errand and has asked her to give me directions to the house, which she does. I ask if there is anything I can pick up for her, since I will be traveling through town to get to the house. "Oh, no thank you. We have everything we need. Do you drink coffee? I'll have a cup ready for you when you get here if you do," she responds.

"I'm not a coffee drinker," I tell her, "but I'd love a glass of ice water."

I park on one side of the wide driveway of a very nice single story ranch home, located in a small, affluent residential area sandwiched among a local school complex, the Cleveland Country Club, and Delta State University, a college of 4,000 students, where "Boo" coached baseball for 26 years after his retirement from the Red Sox. As I get out of the car, Miriam opens the door at the side of the carport and invites me to come in. "Dave should be back in just a few minutes. Please come in and sit down and I'll get that glass of water you wanted."

Knowing that I am from outside the area, Miriam asks what my impression is of Mississippi. I tell her of my familiarity with the area from having traveled it frequently as a salesman living in Memphis back in the late '60s. She expresses her extreme displeasure with the gambling casinos that now operate along the Mississippi River near Tunica. "I just think all of those casino signs along the highway look so tacky. And they bring people in here by the busloads to throw away their money, and I can't see where the state of Mississippi has anything to show for it."

While Miriam and I are talking, "Boo" arrives, shakes my hand while introducing himself, and sits down in the corner of the large sofa opposite me in the family room. He asks how I started with my hobby and I recite the story for him.

"Tell me how you got the name 'Boo'," I inquire.

"Well, it goes back to my early childhood. I had an older brother named Bobby and whenever I tried to say his name, I could only say 'Boo.' So, everyone started calling ME 'Boo' and the nickname just stuck. I've been going by 'Boo' ever since."

We talk about some of "Boo's" teammates, many of whom he has seen at recent get togethers of the 1946 Red Sox team. He speaks fondly of Bobby Doerr, whom he and Miriam visit occasionally, Ted Williams, and Tom McBride, who lives in Wichita Falls, TX. "You should go up to see McBride. He'll sign your bat. Tell him I told you to come see him."

I notice that "Boo" has a somewhat distracting habit of yawning every couple of minutes. It does not seem to be a yawn born of fatigue or disinterest, but merely a physical anomaly. I am initially a little uncomfortable, thinking perhaps my presence is an imposition, but soon realize that "Boo" is enjoying talking with me and that the yawning is just part of his persona.

"What are some of the best memories of your career as a ballplayer?" I ask.

"I'll never forget a day in 1941. It was before I actually got to the major leagues. I had been pitching summer ball in a prospect league up in Vermont. When our season was finished, the Red Sox invited me to spend 10 days with them to help pitch batting practice. They took me with the team on a trip to New York to play the Yankees and one day I watched Ted Williams hit 3 consecutive home runs off Lefty Gomez in one game. You know, Gomez was a pretty good pitcher, but that day Williams made it look like Lefty was throwing it up there about 75 miles an hour. Of course, that was the year Ted hit .406. Then, of course, 1946 was a great year for us. We started the season by winning something like 41 of our first 50 games and wound up in the World Series against the Cardinals."

"Boo" and Miriam both speak about how pleasant it was to be in the Red Sox organization. They speak of the "family" atmosphere that was a part of the Red Sox teams in the years when they were with the team and talk about how many of "Boo's" teammates spent their entire career with the Red Sox. Clearly, there seems to be a mutual loyalty in the minds of the Ferrisses, as Miriam remarks, "It wasn't like today, when everyone just goes to play for whoever is offering the most money. We had sort of a family and we still feel a part of that family today."

As I thank them and prepare to leave, "Boo" offers to tell me a short-cut back to the highway. Miriam chimes in, "Oh

'Boo,' don't get him confused now, he knows the way back the way he came."

"Boo" walks me outside and we talk briefly about the rivalry that "Boo's" Delta State baseball teams used to have with the Alabama Southern team, coached by Eddie Stanky. Then, making sure he is out of earshot of his wife, "Boo" smiles and says, 'Want to know about that shortcut?'

I take the new directions and, before leaving, listen to "Boo" talk briefly about some of the teams he coached at Delta State. "We made it to the Division II College World Series a few times. Not too bad for a little school like Delta State. And I sent a couple of kids on to the majors, guys like Donnie Moore. Gene Bearden, who used to pitch for the Indians, lives over in Helena (Arkansas) and used to put me on to some good ballplayers from over in his area."

After thanking "Boo" again, I am on my way to Little Rock (using the shortcut that "Boo" was so anxious to tell me about).

WILLARD MARSHALL
Rockleigh, NJ
March, 1999

Willard lives in a grand old home on a large, gorgeous, tree-studded property in rural Rockleigh. A keystone in the arch over the front door of his home is inscribed with the date 1828. He has lived there with his daughter, her husband, and his two grandsons (ages 12 and 9) since his wife passed away three years ago. According to Sal Yvars, a former teammate of Marshall's, Willard's previous home in Fort Lee, NJ was built on a hill and had a clear and spectacular view of the city of New York from his back yard.

Willard's daughter greets me at the front door and invites me to follow her through the large dining room to a short stairway leading down into a large wood paneled room, which serves as a combination of library and great room. The room has a huge stone fireplace and many built-in bookcases with glass windowed doors. Willard's memorabilia is displayed throughout the room; on the mantle, on the tops of the bookcases, and on the walls. Particularly unique are the uniform caps that he wore with the various teams he played for; two Giants caps, two Boston Braves caps, and a Cincinnati Reds cap. There are team photos and photos from games, banquets, golf tournaments, and other events throughout the room. Among the books that fill the bookcases are many about baseball.

Welcoming me with a handshake, Willard invites me to "make myself at home" with a seat on the large overstuffed sofa that faces the fireplace, as he returns to his easy chair facing me. He is dressed as though ready to play golf, wearing a green MLBPAA (Major League Baseball Players' Alumni Association) sweater over a yellow shirt. He still has the substantial head of wavy hair that I recall from his playing days. He immediately impresses me as a classic "southern gentleman."

I ask Willard if he sees much of his former teammates.

"Oh, I mostly see them now and then at the local golf outings sponsored by MLBPAA and at banquets, but my legs have been giving me a lot of trouble lately, so I don't get around as much as I used to. I used to play a lot of golf, but I can't play anymore. I have pretty much constant pain in my legs and sometimes they just collapse on me when I'm walking. I see Buddy Kerr and Sal Yvars once in awhile. Buddy lives right over in Oradell.

Willard asks me to "fill him in" on any of his teammates that I have seen lately. He asks if I know anything about Montia Kennedy, whom he knows has been seriously ill at his home near Richmond. I am surprised to hear this, as I am planning to try to visit Kennedy later in the week. Willard asks me to let him know if I am able to find anything out about Kennedy's condition.

"You know, Willard, I remember going to a Sunday doubleheader in Cincinnati with my dad and brother when I was a kid. The Reds were playing the Dodgers and we sat in the right field bleachers. It was the only time I ever sat in the bleachers at Crosley Field. My dad always said that the two best arms in the National League belonged to you and Carl Furillo, so we sat out there to be able to watch you play. As I recall, the two of you threw out a total of seven baserunners in that doubleheader. I'll never forget that," I tell him.

"Well, I always had a very accurate arm, but I think Furillo had a much stronger arm," he responds.

"Who was the best manager you played for?" I ask.

"As a human being, I liked Paul Richards best. As a baseball manager, I think Leo Durocher would be hard to beat. He didn't play any favorites. All he wanted to do is WIN!"

"What about pitchers? Who did you like to hit against and who gave you the most trouble?"

"I always seemed to hit Ewell Blackwell well. I was able to pick up the ball real early with him. The guys who gave me a lot of trouble were Al Brazle, the St. Louis lefthander, and probably Erskine of the Dodgers, with that overhand curve ball."

We chat about several players from his day and Willard comments that the only players he ever had any trouble getting along with were Ferris Fain and Dave Koslo. "Ferris had a really strange personality. He was very unpredictable and volatile. He could get upset with something that was said very innocently and take it as a personal matter. I said something quite casually in a card game on the train one time and Ferris didn't speak to me for the rest of the season and we were teammates, you know. He finally came over to me after the last game of the season and apologized, but he was a very difficult fellow to figure. Dave Koslo was a little bit the same way, but I got along fine with everyone else in the game."

As I prepare to leave, Willard tells me about some of the pictures on the wall and shows me some more that are displayed in the huge living room, We talk a little more about the house and he tells me he doesn't know how long they will keep it. His daughter is in the real estate business, he says, and she is interested in "testing the market" to see what it might bring. He tells me to feel free to stop by anytime I may be in the area again and reminds me to pass his greetings along to any old teammates that I might visit later, especially Montia Kennedy, whom he seems genuinely concerned about.

I subsequently learned that Montia Kennedy had passed away two years earlier, in March, 1997.

Willard Marshall passed away on November 5, 2000.

SAL YVARS
Valhalla, NY
March, 1999

Sal Yvars must surely be one of baseball's best storytellers. His stories are mostly about bizarre happenings, and Sal swears that every one of them is true. As Sal and I sit in the living room of the Yvars home, we are joined by Sal's wife, Ann, who gives me a glass of water and sits down to listen to our conversation. I ask Sal if he sees many of his old teammates and that is all it takes to get him started.

"I see a lot of the fellows who live near New York, not just baseball guys, but guys from all sports at the golf outings and banquets that go on all the time. I love to play golf, so I don't miss a chance to get out with the guys and play. I do some banquet speaking from time to time and I'm supposed to have a book coming out. One night after I spoke at a banquet, a guy came up to me and told me he wanted to publish a book based upon the stories I had told during the banquet. I spent three months recording the stories on tape for him and when I had finished he said, 'This is great, Sal, but we need a few stories with some sex in them.' I absolutely went berserk! I asked the guy why in the hell he had wasted three months of my time, and his, if all he wanted was for me to dump some garbage on my friends and teammates. Anyway, someone else has the tapes now and I don't know whether it will ever get published or not."

Sal continues, "The title of the book was to be The Year The Giants Stole The Pennant. It was about the 1951 pennant race when we came back from 13 ½ games down to beat the Dodgers in a playoff. People don't believe it, but here's what actually happened. Late in the summer, when it looked like we had no chance of getting back into the pennant race, Leo (Durocher) ran into a friend of his who was connected with the Navy in some way. He told Leo that the Navy had a high-powered telescope that could spot a crystal of ice on the surface of the ocean from some fantastic distance. He told Leo he could get one of the telescopes and install it in the clubhouse in centerfield at the Polo Grounds and be able to steal the opposing catcher's signals. So we did it and knew almost every pitch that an opposing pitcher was going to throw when we were playing at home."

"But Sal, how could you get the information to the batter in time to do him any good?" I ask.

"We had a line wired from the clubhouse to a buzzer in our dugout and one in our bullpen, which was located in right-center field. The batter had a clear view to the bullpen. One of our players, often myself, would sit at one end of the bullpen bench and pass the signals. One buzz meant a fastball, two a breaking ball or off-speed pitch, and three a knockdown. The player passing the signs would have a ball in his hand. If the signal was for a fastball, the player giving the signal would just sit in place. If a curveball was coming, he would toss the ball in the air a few times. If a knockdown was coming, and there were LOTS of knockdowns when we played the Dodgers, the player would stand up. Like I said, people don't believe the story, but it's true. If you look at our record in the Polo Grounds during the last part of 1951, you'll see we didn't lose many games and it's because we literally STOLE the opponent's signals and the pennant with that telescope. We went on to win the pennant on Bobby Thomson's miracle home run and lost to the Yankees in six games in the World Series. I made the last out in the Series. I've always said, 'Bobby got us in and I got us out.'"

"Sal, I have never understood why Dressen used Branca to pitch against Thomson in that last playoff game, when Thomson had hit Branca hard two days earlier, including a home run," I comment.

"It wasn't Dressen's choice," Sal replies. "Branca and Erskine were warming up. Dressen called to the bullpen and asked the bullpen coach who was ready and was told that Branca was ready, so that's who he used."

"You talked about the knockdown pitch. Tell me some more about that," I say.

"Well, the knockdown was a routine part of the game when we were playing. Of course, Sal Maglie was one of the best with the knockdown. Maglie was actually a very nice and mild sort of person, but he was a master at the trade of pitching and the knockdown was an important part of his pitching repertoire. He used it to set up his other pitches and to send 'messages' to opposing batters. He was Willie Mays' protector. Of course, when we played the Dodgers, because of the intense rivalry, knockdowns were an important part of game strategy. For example, you could pretty well eliminate Furillo and Campanella as batting threats by knocking them down. It definitely made them less aggressive in the batter's box. On the other hand, some players, like "PeeWee" (Reese) and Jackie (Robinson), became MORE aggressive and dangerous if you knocked them down."

Sal continues, "I remember a time when Reese baited me perfectly. I was catching and, when Reese stepped into the batter's box, I noticed that he was crowding the plate a little, like he was looking for a curveball away. So, I signaled for a fastball inside. The pitch was thrown perfectly, right where I wanted it, and that little shit just stepped back with his left leg and hammered the ball into left field for a hit. He knew exactly what he was doing and what I was going to do."

At some point during our conversation, Ann has left the room and gone to the kitchen. She returns and announces, "Come on you two, lunch is on the table. You can talk some more after lunch."

I try to decline lunch, but Sal and Ann will not permit me to leave. There are sandwich rolls and a plate full of cheese and sandwich meats on the table. When I am about finished building a modest salami and swiss cheese sandwich, Sal reaches over, takes the top piece of bread from my sandwich, and stacks more salami and cheese on it. "C'mon, don't be so damned polite! Put some meat on that thing!" he insists. Nor does he allow me to decline the Breyer's butter pecan ice cream for dessert.

After lunch we resume our conversation in the living room. Sal wants to tell me about Leo Durocher and "Jocko" Conlon, an umpire.

"Leo and 'Jocko' were always going at it with one another. One day (Wes) Westrum was injured and couldn't play, so I was going to catch. 'Jocko' was the home plate umpire that day and Leo knew it wasn't uncommon for me to take issue with umpires. So, he goes to 'Jocko' before the game and says, 'Look, Yvars is the only catcher I have today, so whatever you do, please don't throw him out of the game.'"

"Well, things go along okay until about the sixth inning and 'Jocko' calls a pretty good pitch a ball and I say something to him about it. He says, 'Shut up Yvars! You catch and I'll umpire.' A little later he makes another questionable call and I'm on him again. This time he says, 'One more word out of you and I'm giving you the rest of the day off.' On the very next pitch we get into it again and he erupts, 'That's it Yvars! You're outa' here!' Now here comes Leo out of the dugout, running up to home plate, pushing me out of the way, and pleading with Conlon, 'C'mon Jocko, you can't throw him out. For Christ's sake, he's the only catcher I've got. Let him finish and he won't say another word.' And by golly he let me finish the game."

When I'm ready to leave, Sal goes to the dining room and returns with several small photographs and hands them to me. "Here, take these with you," he commands. He then insists upon taking his car and leading me back to the highway that will take me to the Tappan Zee Bridge. He will not let me decline the offer. When he leaves for the garage to get his car, I tell Ann, "Ann, I can find my way back. He doesn't need to do that."

"Oh, don't worry about it. He needs to get out for a while and I could use a little time to myself. It's no problem," she assures me.

As I say goodbye and thank Ann for lunch and her hospitality, Sal backs his car out of the garage. He is smoking a big cigar. With the cigar in his mouth and a big smile on his face, Sal motions with a grand sweep of his arm for me to follow him. A few minutes later, he motions me onto the highway ramp and waves goodbye.

ALLIE CLARK
South Amboy, NJ
March, 1999

Allie and his wife, Fran, live in an upstairs apartment in South Amboy. Allie has told me that they are leaving for Florida the following morning, so I must get there today or wait until another time to meet him. When I arrive, Fran meets me at the back door, which opens into the kitchen. "Come on in. I saw you coming. Allie will be back in a few minutes. We can wait in the living room. Would you like something to drink?"

"A glass of ice water would be fine, thank you," I reply.

Fran brings me a glass of water, leads me into the living room, and invites me to sit on the sofa. Quickly scanning the room, I spot an open suitcase on the floor of the living room. It is packed, ready for an imminent departure. While we wait for Allie, Fran tells me about the trip they took last year to Cleveland to celebrate the 50th anniversary of the Indians'

1948 World Championship. Clark was an outfielder on that team. She speaks of how few of the team members are still alive and of how much she enjoyed seeing Steve Gromek and his wife again after so many years. While she is talking, I hear the door in the hall open and Allie walks in. He is husky in stature, has a pleasant round face, and thrusts his hand out in greeting. "You got here sooner than I thought. I was getting ready to have another beer at the tavern," he says with a smile.

"Well, let's go. I'll have one with you," I reply.

He laughs and motions me to sit down and asks what it is I want him to sign.

"You know, I'm one of only eight players who ever played on consecutive world championship teams, with different teams. I was on the 1947 New York Yankees and then, in 1948, with the Cleveland Indians. Matter of fact, last year we went to a reunion up in Cleveland for that '48 team," Allie advises. "When we get back from Florida, I'll be going to a shindig put on by the Philadelphia A's Historical Society," Allie adds, handing me a copy of the Society's Newsletter announcing the event and telling me to keep it.

Allie is proud of the fact that he has overcome some serious health problems. He has had bypass surgery and also had to deal with a cancer problem in his neck, in some respects similar to my own problem in 1982, although Allie's involved more extensive surgery. He also has an ongoing fight with skin cancer from extensive past exposure to the sun. He comments on the issue, "I can't complain when I look around at all my former friends and teammates who have passed away. All in all, I guess I'm doing okay."

Before I leave, Allie gives me three photos to add to my collection and invites me to return anytime I am in the area.

JOE MOORE **"The Gause Ghost"**
Bryan,TX
April, 1999

At age 90, "Jo-Jo" Moore claims to be the oldest living New York Giant. He played on Giant teams in the 1933, '36, and '37 World Series and earned a place in the World Series record book by having 2 hits in a single inning and by having 9 hits in a 5 game Series (a record which has been tied). He claims to have played most of his career at a playing weight of 145 pounds and was known for his speed, hence, his nickname "The Gause Ghost". He lives alone on the third floor of a retirement home in Bryan, his wife having died five years ago, but he still drives and frequently visits his son, who lives 45 minutes away in Gause. As might be expected, Joe's hand is shaky, but he is a willing signer.

Joe and I talk about Harry Danning, who first suggested I visit Moore, and recall some of the baseball stories that Danning had told me. In recalling the incident that involved the ejection of Moore, Danning, and Jurges by three different umpires over the same play, a disputed home run by Harry Craft in Cincinnati, Moore adds, "That play probably cost us the pennant, because Jurges was suspended for 15 days for spitting at Magerkurth. In those days you didn't mess around with Commissioner Landis. None of that stuff like a year or so ago when that guy (Roberto Alomar) spit at the umpire and had his suspension delayed until the next year. Judge Landis would have had his ass right then and there! No questions asked! No excuses!"

"What do you remember best about your playing days?" I ask.

"Well, the first pitcher I ever faced in the big leagues was 'Dizzy' Dean. He was a pretty tough guy to break in against, but all the pitchers were tough in those days. There weren't so many teams then and the fellows who made it to the 'bigs' were plenty tough. We usually had good games against Dean though, because Carl Hubbell usually pitched against Dizzy. Carl was a helluva' pitcher. Give him one run and he'd make it stand up. Give him ten runs and he'd give up nine and wear his fielders out chasing balls all over the park! It seemed like, no matter what, Carl could pitch just good enough to win."

Joe adds a comment about Joe DiMaggio. "I think DiMaggio really rejuvenated the Yankees in 1936. His presence on that team (which defeated Moore's Giants in the '36 World Series) made a big difference. He seemed to bring a new sense of pride and purpose to the team. His personality was a bit strange, to be sure, but he got that organization going again."

Joe shows me a ball autographed by Franklin Roosevelt that he claims is the ball that FDR threw out as the first pitch at the 1933 All-Star Game, an article written by Ira Berkow in the Christmas Day 1998 issue of the New York Times (in honor of Joe's 90th birthday on that date), and an old Giants yearbook featuring the Giants Hall of Fame, which includes Joe Moore. He tells me that I might want to look up Bill Lohrman, a former teammate who is still living somewhere in New York, and then takes me to another room where he keeps his own memorabilia, mostly books, an aging scrapbook, and a ball autographed by Charlie Gehringer.
As I prepare to leave, Joe wishes me well and asks me to pass his regards along to Harry Danning, if I should see him again.

Joe Moore passed away April 1, 2001.

ERNIE KOY
Bellaire, TX
April, 1999

Few families can claim the athletic legacy of the Koy family. I knew, of course, that Ernie had played for the Dodgers and the Reds in the '30s, but, somehow, I had failed to connect his name with a more recent history of athletic achievement by other members of his family. My visit with Ernie was pleasantly enlightening in this regard.

Ernie and his wife are pulling out of their carport, on their way to the store, when I pull into the driveway. When he sees my car, Ernie stops, gets out of the car with his wife, and the two of them introduce themselves to me. Mrs. Koy tells Ernie to take me on into the house while she goes to the store alone. Their home is a lovely single story brick in a heavily treed upscale residential area. Ernie says that eleven doctors live in the immediate neighborhood. Ernie tells me to bring the items I want him to sign into the house and suggests we sit at the dining room table.

Entering the dining room, I notice a current photo of a University of Texas football player, in a passing pose, on the buffet table. "Is that your grandson?" I ask.

"Yes, he's going to be a quarterback. Several of our family members have played at Texas," he replies.

Suddenly, it dawns on me! The great Koy running backs of the highly successful Longhorn teams of the '60s are Ernie's sons! Ernie himself played at Texas from 1930-32. Ernie, Jr. played from 1962-64 and was a running back on the 1963 national championship team. He went on to play in the NFL with the New York Giants. Then followed Ted Koy, who played from 1967-69. He was a running back on the 1969 national championship team and also played in the NFL for the Buffalo Bills. Ernie shows me a piece from a UT football program, confirming this history. He tells me that, in addition to his grandson at UT, he has two other grandsons, one at Harvard, one at the Naval Academy, and a granddaughter who is an All-American basketball player at Rice. Clearly, the Koy family is a remarkably athletic one!

Ernie doesn't talk a lot about his baseball career. He is humble and soft spoken and prefers to talk about his sons and grandchildren, for obvious reasons. But he does make mention of the fact that he did not care at all for Leo Durocher. "Leo was a loudmouth. One day when I was playing left field and Leo was at shortstop, a high pop fly was hit into short left field. I had an easy play on the ball, but Leo kept yelling that he had it. So, I came off the ball to let him take it and he let it drop. After the inning was over, in the dugout, he kept bitching that I should have caught the ball. I got tired of hearing him mouth off, so I just went over to him and punched him right in the chops! I didn't have any more trouble with him, but three years later they made him the manager and the first thing he did was trade me to St. Louis! That's the sort of guy Leo Durocher was."

As I prepare to leave, I tell Ernie that Joe Moore asked me to say "hello" and to stop and see him if he gets over to Bryan. Ernie asks for a report on Joe and comments that he really should get over to see Joe. He suggests the best route for returning to Houston, walks me out to the car, and thanks me for stopping to see him.

ED STEVENS
Houston, TX
April, 1999

As Ed Stevens tells it, he is forever linked to Jackie Robinson's entry into major league baseball in 1947. Sitting in the living room of his home in an upper middle class suburb in southwest Houston, Ed tells me a story that he obviously feels great passion about. His wife, Margie, who has just finished telling me of the recent and untimely death of their 52 year old daughter from an undiagnosed coronary occlusion, excuses herself from the room. She has heard Ed's story many times.

"When Branch Rickey brought Jackie to the Dodgers in 1947, I was 22 years old, had recently made the team, and was going to be the first baseman. Of course, when the season started, Jackie played first base. About a month into the season we were playing in Cincinnati and Mr. Rickey called me to a meeting in a taxicab outside the stadium. I was in uniform, getting ready to take batting practice, when he called for me, so I went to the cab, in uniform, to meet him. He told me that I was a Brooklyn Dodger and a member of his team and that he needed a favor from me. The team rosters were being reduced and he needed a spot for Jackie. He told me I was his youngest player and he wanted me to agree to go to Montreal for a month or so. He said he was planning to trade Eddie Stanky (Dodger second baseman at the time), move Jackie to second, and bring me back to play first base. I didn't particularly like the idea, but in those days a man's word was his bond, so I went to Montreal. At Montreal that year, I led the league in home runs and RBIs, but Rickey didn't call me back to Brooklyn until the rosters were expanded at the end of the year. Even then, he did so three days after the cutoff date that would have qualified me for the World Series roster and a World Series share. Then, at the end of the season, he traded me to Pittsburgh. Now, here's the irony! When I retired from baseball I was 42 days short of the number required for earning pension benefits and Jackie Robinson's uniform number was 42!"

"It took a long time for me to get those 42 days. Billy Martin assured me many times that he would get me a coaching job as soon as he could land a manager's job, but every time he got a job he told me the club was naming his coaches. I lost all respect for him over that. Jack McKeon and Eddie Brinkman were the guys who finally helped me get those 42 days. Brinkman was a coach for McKeon with the San Diego Padres and he gave up his coaching spot to let me get 44 days as an active coach on a major league roster, which gave me the time I needed for my pension. It was a very nice thing for him to do."

Ed loved playing in Pittsburgh. He says he was a fan "favorite," and he was never booed in Pittsburgh. "The fans would get on some of the players if they weren't doing well, but they always were behind me, no matter how I was playing," he says.

Ed's hand is a little shaky as he signs my bats. He stops to show me how his thumb twitches when he holds a pen. He tells me how a promoter from New York, who does private signings with the old Brooklyn Dodgers, had been to his home a few weeks before. "This guy shows up in a big van and starts unloading all this stuff for me to sign. He arrived at 9:00 in the morning and I was signing stuff until 6:00 that evening! Of course, we were talking and stopped for some lunch, but I never signed so much stuff in my life. It was a real circus! I don't mind signing things for people like you who have a collection, but when someone is going to be selling something that I have signed, like a dealer, then I expect to be paid."

Before I leave, Ed shows me his own memorabilia collection, an extensive display of both posed and action photos from his playing career in Brooklyn and Pittsburgh, which is displayed on all four walls of a reading room, just off the living room. He thanks me for visiting and invites me to return anytime that I'm in the area.

MIKE GOLIAT
Seven Hills, OH
April, 1999

Mike has just finished cutting the grass at his suburban Cleveland home when I arrive. He is getting ready to clean up and put his mower away in the garage. He has a full head of snow white hair and walks out of the garage and greets me with a smile and a handshake.

After talking for a while about some of his teammates on the 1950 Philadelphia Phillies ("Whiz Kids"), many of whom have passed away in recent years, he comments about his own short career in the majors: "When I came up as an infielder, I had played at first, second, and third base. Third was my best position, but I wasn't going to replace Willie Jones at third and Eddie Waitkus was pretty well established at first, so I wound up playing second. In my first game with the Phillies, I got my knee torn up on a double play pivot at second base. The injury never really completely healed and, as a result, I lost that quick first step that is so important to an infielder. So, I didn't have a very long career, but that 1950 season was a real dream."

Mike isn't too impressed with the state of the game today. "Today they have so many teams that the talent just isn't there. Most teams are lucky if they have more than one or two good pitchers. When we played, you faced a good pitcher every day! We had Robin Roberts, Curt Simmons, Bob Miller, and Russ Meyer to start, and then we had Jim

Konstanty for relief. And we were not considered to have the best pitching staff in the league. Even at that, today you have guys who can't hit .250 that make a million dollars a year! It's a joke!"

Mike tells me a little bit about his family. He is particularly proud of his 16 year old granddaughter, Kelly Goliat, who he says is destined to become a champion figure skater. "She practices hard every day. Keep your eyes out for her in a couple of years. I think you'll see her doing well in some major competition."

Mike says he has to leave to go start cutting the grass at his son's eight-acre farm, so I excuse myself, thank him for allowing me to visit, and leave.

Mike Goliat died January 14, 2004.

ELROY FACE
North Versailles, PA
April, 1999

Elroy's wife greets me at the door of the Face's second story apartment, located behind a nursing home in suburban Pittsburgh. "Elroy's in the shower, but he'll be out in a few minutes. Come on in."

Mrs. Face obviously loves cardinals. Her collection of ceramic cardinals is displayed throughout the living room. There are also a few drawings and photos of cardinals, as well as a flag featuring a cardinal on the deck outside. When I comment about the display, she boasts, "Oh, I also have a couple of Cardinal baseball jackets. One of them was sent to me by Joe Torre when he was a manager or coach with the Cardinals."

She takes a moment to show me the framed lithograph of Elroy that was presented to him recently in conjunction with his induction into the Ted Williams Hall of Fame in Florida. She is obviously quite proud of it.

Elroy enters the living room buttoning his Fox TV Network shirt. His hair is tousled and still wet from his shower. He smiles and offers his hand in greeting. For one so short in stature, Elroy has unusually large hands and long fingers. They are features that helped him become so successful throwing the rapidly sinking "forkball" that made him one of the game's most effective relief pitchers.

"Elroy, tell me about the forkball," I say.

He grins broadly and offers the following story. "Lou Brock came up to me one day when he was playing with the Cardinals and told me that Bruce Sutter, who was a Cardinals relief pitcher at the time, had come to him one day in the clubhouse and was showing Lou how he gripped his split-fingered fastball."

"It's the same pitch that Elroy Face called his forkball," Sutter said.

Brock responded, "No it's not! I can hit yours and I couldn't hit Elroy's!"

Elroy talks about his recent induction into the Ted Williams Hall of Fame. He says Ted attended the ceremony, but made his appearance in a wheelchair. He tells me he has some extra copies of the lithograph that is displayed on the wall and offers me one for $25, a price that is considerably less than dealers in the Pittsburgh area are charging. Admiring the work, I accept his offer and he autographs the piece for me.

I thank Elroy and his wife for letting me stop by and head across town to meet Frank Thomas.

FRANK THOMAS
North Hills, PA
April, 1999

When I called Frank to ask him if he would autograph a couple of bats for my collection, he was quite willing to do so, but wanted me to know that he charged $20 per bat and that he donates all of the fee to a charity for children with life threatening diseases.

Frank lives in a lovely two story home in an affluent suburb on the north side of Pittsburgh. Answering the door, he asks me in and tells me he needs to finish a phone call. A few minutes later, he invites me into the breakfast room, where we sit at the table and he immediately begins signing the two bats that I have brought in. His manner is somewhat businesslike. As he signs the bats, he explains, "I give all my signing fees to two organizations that are very much like Grant A Wish. They are for children who are suffering from cancer and the money goes toward providing them with experiences that they otherwise would be unable to have. Jim Greengrass, Mel Parnell, and I have been supporting them for many years."

After signing the bats, Frank tells me that his Topps baseball card collection, from all of the years that he was active as a player, was lost in a fire in his home in 1991. He is trying to rebuild the collection and asks if I have any cards from that era. I tell him that I have some duplicates to a 1954 Topps set and would be glad to let him know what I have. He leaves the room for a short time and returns and hands me a four page list of card numbers that he is trying to find. Many have been checked off. I tell him I will send him anything I have that he is missing.

He takes me into the living room to show me his substantial display of autographed baseballs, most of which are displayed in a specially built glass front case. There is also an enlarged cover of a Sports Illustrated cover featuring Frank, and a set of engraved plaques detailing every home run he hit in his major league career, the date, the park, and the pitcher he hit it against. He tells me that Monte Irvin arranged to have the plaques made for him. He also shows me two Sosnak baseballs that were painted by the famous baseball artist commemorating Frank's career.

I ask Frank which pitchers gave him the most trouble and which ones he most liked to hit against.

"Drysdale was awfully tough on right-handed hitters. I guess he gave me the most trouble. I used to hit Newcombe, Antonelli, and Haddix pretty well…and Paul Minner. I got my first big league hit off Minner and I pretty much 'owned' him. One time he hit me in the backside with a pitch and as I was going down to first base he looked at me, laughed, and said, 'I thought for once that I'd hit you before you hit me!'"

Upon entering the living room, I can't help noticing a large color family portrait that includes 20-25 members of several generations of the Thomas family. I comment on the portrait and ask Frank if that is his entire family.

"Yes, everyone is there except our 17 year old daughter, whom we lost tragically many years ago," Frank replies.

"What happened to her?" I ask.

"She was at a New Year's Eve party at a hotel with a group of her high school friends and an elevator she and several of

the kids were on got stuck between floors. The kids managed to pry the doors open part way and were trying to get down onto the floor below. Somehow, a piece of her clothing caught on the elevator and she fell three stories down the elevator shaft to her death."
I groan audibly and express my sympathy.

"They had to do an autopsy, because of the circumstances, but found no evidence of alcohol or anything that would have contributed to the accident. It was just a really weird thing," he concludes.

Leaving the living room, Frank takes the opportunity to express his frustration and displeasure with baseball's Hall of Fame. "It's a political thing. If you look at the percentage of Hall of Famers who played on teams in proximity to the New York market, you get an idea of how the system works. I had a few accomplishments in my career, but nobody from the Hall of Fame has ever asked for anything of mine. When I played in Milwaukee, Eddie Mathews, Hank Aaron, Joe Adcock, and I hit consecutive home runs in one inning and they didn't even ask me for my bat. I guess it really doesn't matter. I know what I accomplished, whether they choose to recognize it or not."

"What are your thoughts about Pete Rose?" I ask.

"I like Pete, but Pete knew that the league would provide help for anyone with an addiction of any sort. The policy is prominently displayed on the door of every clubhouse in baseball. Pete chose to ignore the policy and not to seek help. He thought he was above the rules. So, it's difficult for me to be overly sympathetic toward Pete, although, if players' off the field activities are really a criteria, there are lots of fellows who don't belong in there. Just stop and think of the players now in the Hall of Fame who had documented problems with drugs, alcohol, gambling, and all sorts of things." He names several examples.

Although Frank has a rather serious and direct personality, I have enjoyed my visit with him. As he walks me outside, he tells me that, in addition to maintaining his own substantial yard and shrubbery, he maintains the yards for several of his neighbors. "I've been doing it for years and now most of them are old enough that they couldn't afford to have someone else do it, if I decided not too. My wife isn't too happy about it, but that's the way I feel about it, so I just keep doing it."

I ask him to give my regards to Willard Marshall, whom Frank will see at a card show in New Jersey the coming weekend, and leave.

A few weeks later, I received a letter from Frank, dated 20 April 1999. It reads, in part, "I wanted to write to tell you that I just got back from the card show in New Jersey. Willard Marshall called in Thursday. I should say his daughter called and said that Willard came down with a virus and he couldn't see. She was crying on the phone, the men who promoted the show told me. That is all I could find out from the promoter. That hit me like a ton of bricks. Goes to show you, spend every day as if it is your last. Jack, again thanks and I enjoyed meeting you. Let me hear from you. Sincerely, (signed) Frank."

BOB FRIEND **"Pitch"**
Fox Chapel, PA
April, 1999

"Pitch," as he is known to his family and close friends, meets me outside an Eckard's drug store in a small strip mall in Fox Chapel. It is a miserable day, chilly and raining, and neither of us really wants to spend a lot of time in such nasty conditions. We sit down on a small bench under a canopy at the front of the store and “Pitch” signs 2 bats for me.

Looking at the autographs on the bats, he comments, “Gee, you really get around, don’t you! How do you find all these guys?”

I tell him about Jack Smalling’s address book (The Baseball Autograph Collector’s Handbook) and how I tie-in most of my visits with business travel that takes me to most parts of the country.

“Well, it looks like you’re having a lot of fun with it,” he says. “Who else are you planning to see while you’re in town?”

I tell him I’ve visited with Elroy Face and Frank Thomas and hope to be able to see Bobby Del Greco on my way to the airport.

“I see him at a lot of the games,” he says, then adds, “I’m sorry to rush, but I think I want to get out of this lousy weather.” He gets up and prepares to return to his car.

I thank him for arranging to meet me and for signing the bats.

“That’s okay. Glad I could help. Good luck with your hobby.” He shakes my hand and heads for his car.

ROMAN MEJIAS
Los Angeles, CA
April, 1999

Roman’s phone number is unlisted, so I take a chance on catching him at home in a suburb of Los Angeles that most people would probably not choose to visit. Not quite so forbidding as south central LA, the neighborhood just east of Baldwin Park is, nevertheless, not an area one is easily comfortable in. Security is clearly a concern and most of the small homes on the block, including Roman's, have iron bars on the windows. The homes on the block are small, modest, and mostly single story frame houses. Roman's home is surrounded by a recently painted, waist high, old iron fence. The gate is unlocked and the yard is remarkable for the delightful assortment of very well kept flower gardens. The elevated front porch is screened-in and the door providing access has iron bars and is locked. I press the buzzer.

There is no prompt response and, thinking that perhaps nobody is home, I turn to leave. As I do so, the door opens and Roman appears in a pair of work pants, a T-shirt, and a painter's cap. He has been in the back yard working in his flower gardens. I explain the reason for my visit and apologize for not being able to contact Roman by phone to request permission to stop by. He smiles and walks to the porch door. In broken English he says, "Let me see what it is that you have." There is a small door in the middle of the porch door, sort of a "pass through" opening, which Roman opens and gestures me to let him see one of the bats I want him to sign. I pass my Forbes Field bat through the opening to him. He scans the autographs on the bat.

"Ah…Bill Mazeroski! He teach me English when I was at Pittsburgh. He make me learn one new word every day. Very nice man. Very good friend. I am happy to sign the bat with Bill Mazeroski." Roman reaches through the opening in the door for the pen that I have for him to use. He signs two bats and a ball for me. While he is signing, I remark about how nicely kept and beautiful his yard and gardens are. He grins and says, "Yes, I love the flowers."

I ask how he liked playing in Pittsburgh.

"Not so much," Roman says. "One day we have snow and my friend and me can not get up the hill in my car. Some people stop to take us home and when we come back later to get the car, all of the wheels are gone! I no like Pittsburgh very much."

We chat for a short time about baseball, as it was when Roman played, and then it is time to go. I feel very happy to have met and visited with Roman. He is a man of unique pride, as evidenced by the meticulous care that he takes in maintaining his home, his property, and his flowers amidst an otherwise marginally maintained neighborhood. He is a genuinely friendly and appreciative person, the type one wishes the best for.

DINO RESTELLI
San Carlos, CA
April, 1999

This is my third attempt to reach Dino, whose phone number is unlisted. His home appears to house a hermit. The blinds are pulled down over all the windows and the screen door at the front is locked. I'm not sure what to expect as I ring the doorbell again on this, my third visit. I feel some apprehension as I hear someone approach the door and turn the doorknob.

Dino opens the door and, with a kindly smile, asks if he can help me. I explain my mission and he quickly unlocks the screen door and invites me to come in. He is quite pleasant, asks me to have a seat at his dining room table, and tells me he would be happy to sign anything I would like him to. As he signs the Forbes Field bat, he asks me about some of the players whose autographs he recognizes, like Tom Saffell and Pete Castiglione. After signing the items I have for him,

Dino takes me into a hallway off the dining room and shows me several baseball pictures from his playing days.

Returning to the dining room, Dino asks if I need the addresses and phone numbers of other former ballplayers living in the Bay Area. As it turns out, Dino is secretary of the local Baseball Players Alumni Association. He takes out his personal phone directory and starts writing down the names and phone numbers of other former players he thinks I should try to contact. "Oh, these guys love to have the attention. Just tell them I told you to call them. Dempsey lives right up the street. Let's see if he's home. Maybe you can catch him right now."

Dino picks up the phone and dials Con Dempsey's number. Con's daughter answers the phone and tells Dino that Con is out, but should return around dinner time. "Well, just tell him that I'm sending someone up to see him a little later," Dino tells her.

As I thank him for all his help and prepare to leave, Dino asks, "Would you like to have one of my pictures to take for your collection?"

"Sure," I reply.

He leaves the room for a minute and returns with an 8"X10" photo, which he autographs and hands me. As he walks me to the door, he thanks me for stopping by and invites me to return anytime.

My visit with Dino Restelli was one of those totally unexpected pleasures that everyone experiences on occasion. From an initial concern and uncertainty over what to expect at Dino's somewhat foreboding residence came one of the most enjoyable and rewarding visits that I have made, proving that first impressions aren't always correct.

DICK COLE
Costa Mesa, CA
April, 1999

"I was Fred Haney's little 'Bobo'."

That expression, which rolls off Dick Cole's tongue as easily as "Hello" or "How are you?" seems to capture Dick's memories of his major league career. According to Cole and for reasons unknown to him, Haney, at some point in his coaching and managerial career, took a particular liking to him and saw to it that, wherever he went to manage, Dick went with him. He was seldom a "starter," or even a regular player for Haney, but Fred liked having him around as a "utility" player.

"I guess Fred liked the fact that I always worked hard and was an avid student of the game, even when I wasn't playing," Cole asserts. "I played for him at Pittsburgh and when he went on to manage the Milwaukee Braves, he traded for me pretty quickly. That's how I wound up on the Braves World Championship team in 1957. Of course, it didn't hurt that I could play all of the infield positions pretty well."

We are standing in Cole's garage, where he was working when I arrived. He is wiry in build, balding, and taller than I expected. He is still actively involved in baseball, serving as an area scout for the San Francisco Giants in parts of southern California, covering high school and junior college prospects.

"Well, you have a great area to cover," I remark.

"Yes, it should be, but these kids all think they should be millionaires overnight," Dick comments. "They really don't know the game that well, aren't real sharp on fundamentals, and don't want to work very hard. It's kind of a joke, but it keeps me in touch with the game."

I ask, "Do you have any particular memories of your playing days ?"

"Well, I remember one year in spring training playing against the Yankees. I was at shortstop and Manny Fernandez was playing third, and he had a rifle for an arm. Some kid hit a routine grounder to third, Manny fielded it cleanly, took his crow-hop, and threw to first. The kid beat the throw by a step and a half. I'd never seen ANYBODY that fast. It was Mickey Mantle."

Dick says he has to get ready to scout a game, so I thank him for his time and leave.

ED O'BRIEN & JOHNNIE O'BRIEN
Seattle, WA
August, 1999

When I called Ed O'Brien to finalize arrangements for my visit, I asked him for his brother's phone number. Ed suggested that I arrange for the three of us to meet at one time, either at his place or John's, rather than my making separate trips to visit them individually. John was immediately agreeable to meeting at Ed's home on a Saturday morning at 11:00 A.M. "He's got a nicer place than mine," John offered.

Ed O'Brien's home is not particularly large or impressive, except for two very significant points. It is strategically positioned on the side of a hill in Magnolia, a suburb on the northwest side of Seattle, with a totally unobstructed view of the entire downtown Seattle skyline and Puget Sound. The landscaping consists of magnificently planned and maintained gardens with gravel walk paths, a small bench under a magnolia tree, and rocks that Ed's wife, Teri, has collected from around the world. Ed walks me through the entire house, which he and Teri purchased four years earlier, to show me that every room in the house, bathrooms included, has clear views of the spectacular downtown skyline. As we complete the tour, Johnnie and his wife, Jean, arrive. Johnnie has an armful of mail that he puts on the kitchen counter and asks Ed to sign. It is all autograph requests.

"We do things differently," Ed says to me. "I sign stuff the same day I receive it and put it back in the mail. He saves stuff for about a week and then signs it all in a big batch. We get stuff every day and most of it comes from the east coast."

Johnnie sorts through the mail and shows me a check for $10 that someone has sent with an autograph request. "We don't take money for our signatures," he says, "but some show promoters charge a fee when we participate. We usually just get our transportation and lodging paid for."

Johnnie takes the lead when it comes to conversation. "Baseball is in bad shape. The only thing saving it is the home run drama that started last year."

I can't resist responding with an opinion of my own. "Yes, but when you consider the quality of pitching in the game today, the home run thing is sort of a hoax. I mean how many really good pitchers do these guys face in a week?"

"You're right. When we were playing, you faced an ace almost every day. And those guys all knew how to pitch," Ed concedes.

Pitching becomes the focus of our conversation as Johnnie recounts some pitching performances he remembers from his days as a player in the 50's. "Nobody pitches a complete game anymore. I remember talking with Robin Roberts one day when a sportswriter came up and reminded Roberts that, at one point in his career, he had pitched 29 consecutive complete games! Nobody could do that today."

"Another time I remember was when I was with the Pirates. Vern Law pitched 18 innings one night and was tied 1-1 after 18. Bob Friend relieved in the 19th inning and we won 2-1 in the 19th. Friend asked the official scorekeeper to give credit for the "win" to Law, but they couldn't do that. Four days later, Law pitched 13 innings and again left the game in a tie. He pitched 31 innings in four days without a decision!"

"When I was with Milwaukee in '59, Lew Burdette was pitching against the Cardinals when he got in a bases loaded jam late in the game and Stan Musial was coming to bat. Fred Haney (Braves manager) came to the mound to relieve Burdette and Lew would not give him the ball. He told Haney, 'I got myself into this mess and I'll get myself out of it! I'm not turning this situation over to some young kid out of the bullpen.' Haney left the mound and Burdette got Musial to hit into a double play to end the inning."

Johnnie continues. "I remember a game Warren Spahn pitched and won, 2-1, against the Phillies. The Phillies only run came as a result of a two-base hit by Del Ennis with a man on base. It was a pitch that Spahn felt was 'too good' and he shouldn't have thrown to Ennis, a good hitter. When he returned to the dugout at the end of the inning, he threw his glove at the bench and said in disgust, 'Did you see that horse-shit pitch I gave him?' Spahn, like most pitchers of our day, was a perfectionist and worked hard at his skills. I don't see that much today, except maybe with guys like Roger Clemens and those pitchers over in Atlanta (Tom Glavine and Greg Maddux). And look at all the noise they make about pitch counts. What's the big deal? If a guy's in shape, pitch counts shouldn't be necessary. I remember a game Sandy Koufax pitched against us in Pittsburgh. At the end of the article about the game in the paper the next day there was a note mentioning that he had thrown 178 pitches in the course of the game."

Our pitching observations being momentarily exhausted, I change the subject by asking, "Didn't you two get started with basketball?"

Ed takes over on this subject. "That's right! We both played here at the University of Seattle. John was the first player to score 1,000 points during his playing days at Seattle."

Since, at 5'10" I am as tall as either of the O'Briens, I assume that they both played as guards.

"No, actually John played center and I played guard," Ed says.

He then tells me the story of how the two of them, playing high school sports in their hometown of South Amboy, New Jersey, were recruited by the University of Seattle to play basketball. "When we arrived here, the basketball coach and the university president were flabbergasted at our height. It seems as though the fellow who recommended us said that we were both about 6'5". He overestimated by 7 inches. Fortunately, our skills compensated sufficiently for our lack of height and things worked out okay."

Before leaving I take time to visit for a few minutes with Teri and Jean, who have been sitting in an adjacent room visiting while we have been talking baseball. I compliment Teri on her creativity, which is evident not only in the gardens surrounding the house, but in all sorts of other items that Ed has shown me are works of her mind and hands.

My visit here has been a real pleasure and it pleases me to hear the O'Briens say that I am welcome to visit any time I am back in the Seattle area.

GERRY STALEY
Vancouver, WA
August, 1999

Gerry and his wife live in a small, modest, single story house. What would ordinarily be a front yard has been made into an abundant flower garden, which for the most part is in full bloom. The most prominent plantings are purple and white petunias and a beautiful purplish-blue hydrangea.

Gerry and his wife are preparing to leave to attend the stock car races that their son is driving in this afternoon, so my visit with them is somewhat abbreviated. Mrs. Staley is clearly a woman who has enjoyed her husband's career in baseball and she lets it be known quite directly that she doesn't think much of the game or of the players of the present day. Like "Boo" Ferriss's wife, she talks about how close the players and their families were when Gerry was playing. "There was a camaraderie and loyalty among teammates that is missing in today's game. And what about the pitchers today? Does anyone pitch more than 5 innings?" Her words echo my own thoughts on each of the subjects she chooses to address.

Gerry is rather quiet and offers only a few comments about his career, but he makes a point of showing me his collection of very unique baseballs that he displays in the bookcases along one wall of the living room. Each ball commemorates one of his pitching victories while he played for the St. Louis Cardinals and is completely covered with the neatly hand lettered statistics of game details, including date, line score, winning and losing pitchers, hitting highlights, names of umpires, and where the game was played. The printing is meticulously neat. The balls have been superbly preserved with a protective coating of some sort. I have not previously seen anything like this unique collection.

Gerry explains, "Doc Weaver, our trainer with the Cardinals, did those for me after each game that I won when I played for St. Louis."

"Wow! That took some work and a lot of time. Did he do that for all the pitchers?" I ask.

"No, he and I were just good friends and tried to help each other out whenever possible. He did one every now and then for some of the other guys, but he did one for me every time I got a win."

Gerry Staley's baseball collection is so unique that it has to be seen to be appreciated.

LARRY JANSEN
Forest Grove, OR
August, 1999

Larry and his wife live in a farmhouse just north of Forest Grove, a small town about 40 minutes west of Portland. Larry is waiting in the driveway when I arrive and immediately invites me inside. He leads me to the kitchen-breakfast nook, where he introduces me to his wife, who is preparing peaches for canning. She welcomes me as she continues to work. Larry and I sit down at the table, where he promptly signs the two bats and a ball that I have brought in from the car.

After signing, he invites me to take a look at his own collection of memorabilia in the basement. The basement floor is covered with vinyl tile and around two of the walls are numerous pictures from his playing days, many from the 1951 "Shot Heard Round The World" game. The photos are protected by large pieces of plexiglass. Also displayed is an old baseball glove that Larry used in his days as a pitcher in the Pacific Coast League in the 1940s. It is a far cry from today's gloves. There are also some autographed team baseballs on a bookshelf and a family picture with his 10 children, 5 boys and 5 girls.

I ask Larry whether the story I have heard about the telescope in the center field clubhouse at the Polo Grounds is true. He seems a bit annoyed by the question, but his answer is revealing. "Yes, we stole a few signals that way, but most of the signals we stole were from second base," he replies.

I wonder how signals were stolen when there was not a baserunner at second base, but refrain from asking. It is a matter that Larry clearly does not care to pursue, so I change the subject.

"What happened to the (Cleveland) Indians in that 1954 World Series?" I ask.

"Well, they had that great pitching staff and won 111 games that year. I think they took us a little lightly and didn't realize that we had a pretty good bunch of pitchers ourselves. We had Antonelli and Maglie and Ruben Gomez and some other pretty good guys. I think we just sort of surprised them," he responds.

"What are some of the things you most remember about your career?" I ask.

"Well, I was the last pitcher to pitch to Joe DiMaggio. It was the 7th inning of the sixth game of the 1951 World Series and he hit a double to right-center off me. He knew I was going to throw him a slider off the plate and he went out and got it. You know, we talked to the Cleveland pitchers about whether they would rather pitch to DiMaggio or to Ted Williams with men on base and the game on the line. They all said that they would rather pitch to Williams, because he would take the pitch just off the plate and be happy with a base-on-balls, while DiMaggio would anticipate the pitch and go after it in order to try to get the runs in. In that respect, Williams' great eyes and discipline worked against him."

"Who did you have good success against and who gave you the most trouble?" I inquire.

"As far as individuals go, I had good success against Ted Kluszewski. He was an anxious hitter and I knew I could get him out. Perhaps equally important was the fact that Ted knew I could get him out and I usually did. On the other hand, I just could not seem to ever get Ralph Kiner out. He made a living hitting against me. I always had good success pitching against Cincinnati. I think my record against them was something like 27-3, but I don't remember beating the Dodgers in Ebbetts Field. The short left field wall just killed me. Durocher finally decided not to pitch me against Brooklyn and always made sure I was in the rotation against Boston and Cincinnati."

As I am loading the car to leave, I mention the unusual balls that I had seen at Gerry Staley's earlier in the day, the ones done by Doc Weaver.

"Oh, yes! I know what you're talking about. That guy did one of those balls for me when I won my 100th game. Nice guy!"

Larry gives me directions for a short-cut for my return trip to Portland and I am on my way.

CON DEMPSEY
San Carlos, CA
August, 1999

Con's wife invites me into the kitchen to wait for Con, who has just finished showering. She tells me how much Con enjoyed For Love Of The Game, Kevin Costner's new baseball movie, which they had seen together the night before. "I've never seen him so focused watching a movie before," she comments. "He was really into it."

Con walks in, shakes my hand, and picks up on the conversation: "Well, I thought the scenes that dealt with his (Kevin Costner's character) thoughts while pitching the game were quite typical of some of the feelings I experienced as a pitcher. The love story plot was pretty ordinary, but I thought he did a great job of capturing some of the mental part of a ballplayer's experience and I found that to be rather fascinating. It's one of the better movies about baseball that I have seen."

As Con signs the items that I have brought, he comments: "Gee, you've got some great autographs here. I was just in the majors for a 'cup of coffee' as they say. I was a pretty successful young pitcher, but Mr. Rickey wanted to change my pitching style and I wasn't very receptive to his suggestions, so I didn't last very long. I was a ¾-armer and he wanted me to pitch like Vernon Law, my roommate, who was more straight overhand with his delivery. Since I had so much more success with my natural style and resisted his suggestions, Mr. Rickey decided that I was too stubborn to be a successful big league pitcher, so my career was pretty short."

"Mr. Rickey liked having things done his way. Stan Rojek was a young infielder with the Pirates. He was single and led a pretty wild bachelor's life. Mr. Rickey thought that Stan would be a better ballplayer if he would 'settle down.' One day he asked Stan if he had a lady friend. When Stan acknowledged that he did, Mr. Rickey told him that it might be worth a $2,500 addition to his contract if he were to get married. Some time passed before Rojek encountered Mr. Rickey again, but when he did the old man confronted him."

"Did you talk to your lady friend about that proposition I made you?" Mr. Rickey asked.

"I sure did," Stan replied.

"Well?" Rickey queried.

"She told me to hold out for $5,000," Rojek responded.

Con takes considerably more pride in his military record and experience than in his baseball background. He served in both the European and Pacific theaters during WWII as a landing craft operator. He participated in landing operations in both Italy and southern France, before being transferred to the Pacific to assist in the landings at Okinawa. He remembers learning of the war's end.

"I was on Okinawa and we were watching a movie outside, one of those Esther Williams movies or something, when they stopped the projector and announced, 'Gentlemen, the war is over!' I don't think we ever saw the end of that movie."

"You know," Con continues, "none of my children or their spouses seem to understand or appreciate what World War II was all about, or what it means to me to have participated in it. That sort of bothers me, particularly since my daughter-in-law is a native Italian. I made a trip back to Europe not too long ago and visited some of the areas where we had fought and tried to find some of the specific spots that I remembered. When we were in southern France, where I had landed troops 50 years ago, my son suggested I take a jar of the sand from the beach and bring it home, so I did that."

Preparing to leave, I notice a birthday party invitation on the bulletin board in the kitchen. It is for Dino Restelli's 70th birthday. I ask Con to pass my regards on to Dino and make a mental note to get a birthday card in the mail to Dino when I get home.

RON KLINE **"The Callery Hummer"**
Callery, PA
October, 1999

Finding Ron Kline was an adventure. Receiving no response to my letter, having only a rural P.O. Box number for an address, and being unable to obtain Ron's unlisted phone number, I embarked on a mission to find him. I drove to Callery, a very small country town 30 miles or so north of Pittsburgh. Unable to find a town, as such, I stopped at the Blue Moon Saloon, a roadside tavern, near a street sign reading: KLINE. *I approached one of the several patrons in the bar, a man named Ken, and asked, "Is there anyone here who could help me locate Ron Kline?"*

His answer surprised me. "Well, I could probably do that. My name's Ken and Ron lives next door to me," he said matter of factly, and gave me directions to Ron's nearby home!

Knowing that Ron has been ill recently, I ask the young boy who answers the front door not to disturb him when he tells me that Ron is sleeping. Explaining the purpose of my visit and that I had written a note to Ron in advance of my trip and had been unable to obtain the Kline's unlisted phone number, I ask what might be a convenient time for me to call again.

The youth responds confidently, "Oh, I'm sure he won't mind my waking him. He sleeps most of the day. It's not a problem."

Before I can stop him, he walks down a short hall to the back bedroom and I hear his youthful voice explaining my presence. I clearly hear a mature voice respond, "Well, that's okay. Ask him to come on back."

The boy returns and leads me to the bedroom, where Ron is sitting on the edge of the bed. He is wearing pajama bottoms, a white t-shirt, and is breathing oxygen through a nasal canula. His hair is tousled and he appears fatigued. I apologize for disturbing him, but he smiles and extends his hand and says, "It's no problem at all. What do you have that you would like me to sign?"

As he finishes signing the bats and a ball, he says to the young man (probably his grandson), "Ryan, give me a couple of those photographs from the drawer and I'll sign a couple of them for Jack." The photo is from his Pirates playing days. He signs two of them and hands them to me with a smile.

We talk for a few minutes about baseball in the '50s and '60s, when Ron was active in the game. Naturally, he talks about pitching, and his feelings are that pitchers were much better in his day, primarily because major league expansion had not yet taken place. "To pitch in the big leagues then, you had to be pretty good. There were lots of good hitters, particularly in the National League, and a pitcher in those days was expected to pitch nine innings. Of course we had some relievers, but they weren't used like they are today."

I ask Ron about his health problem.

"It's the sugar (diabetes). I just can't get it under control." Extending his left leg so that I can see his substantially swollen left foot, which is covered in a sock, he continues. "They just operated on this one. They did the right one a couple of years ago and the doctor said they probably waited a little too long, so they went ahead on this left one. The problem is that I don't have any feeling in my feet. My skin is also pretty sensitive." He points to skin rashes on his arms and sort of shrugs his shoulders, indicating he doesn't understand it all.

Appreciative of the time Ron has taken to spend with me and aware of his obvious fatigue, I thank him for his hospitality, wish him the best, and leave.

I stopped at the Blue Moon Saloon on my way out of town to thank Ken for helping me locate Ron, and to buy him a beer. It was during this return visit that I learned that the Blue Moon Saloon had at one time been "The Bullpen," a bar that had been jointly owned and operated by Ron Kline and Elroy Face. Needless to say, I will not soon forget my trip to Callery, PA!

Ron Kline passed away June 22, 2002.

BOB PURKEY
Bethel Park, PA
October, 1999

Bob and I had arranged to meet on a Saturday afternoon at his grandson's soccer game in Bethel Park. We had exchanged cellular phone numbers in case problems arose. When rain developed on Saturday, Bob called me to let me know the game had been postponed, but he would be glad to meet with me at a local restaurant. He gave me directions and suggested we meet at 2:00 PM.

Recognizing my car as I pull into the nearly empty parking lot, Bob gets out of his waiting car and motions me to join him as he heads for the entrance to the restaurant. It is a cool, overcast afternoon and a misty rain is falling steadily as I gather the bats that I have and jog to the front door that Bob is holding open for me. Inside there is a large foyer with benches. Bob shakes my hand and suggests that we use the foyer. He opens the door to the restaurant, which is not open for business at this hour, and tells someone that we will be using the foyer for a short meeting. Then he returns, removes his jacket, and sits down on the bench next to me. I mention to him that we have met before at a baseball card show in St. Louis several years ago and he says he recalls doing the show.

Bob is relaxed as he signs three bats for me. He muses over some of the autographs that he sees on each of the bats and makes casual remarks about a few of the players as he reads their names. He chuckles as he reads Frank Thomas's addendum, "The Original One," to his autograph on the Pirates bat. I pick up on his reaction:

"Do you know Frank pretty well?" I ask.

"Yes, I do," Bob replies.

"Isn't it a shame, what happened to his daughter? He told me the story when I was visiting him," I mention.

Bob's mood evolves into one of quiet reflection as he responds. "Yes, it was. You know, Frank was a tremendous source of strength for me when we lost our son, young Bob, not too long after Frank lost his daughter."

"I'm sorry. I didn't know. What happened with your boy?" I inquire.

"Well, it was one of those 'freaky' things, I guess. Bob was a terrific young pitcher. His high school record was 30-0 or 30-1. He was pitching for a junior college team in Florida and they were playing in the junior college world series out in Colorado. The night before the final game, there was a big banquet and I guess they ate a lot of steak and stuff. After dinner, back at the hotel, the guys were having fun around the swimming pool and they were making bets on who could swim the furthest underwater. Bob was a pretty competitive guy, so he jumped in and did a couple of lengths underwater and, when he came up at the end of the pool, he was gasping for air. A couple of guys pulled him out of the pool, but in those days they didn't have all of the emergency equipment that's required now. By the time the life squad arrived, Bob was unconscious. He was in the hospital in a coma for about 10 days and finally passed away."

"Did they ever figure out what happened?" I ask.

"Yes. They had to perform an autopsy and discovered a small defect near the heart. Apparently the stress of the underwater swimming had caused his heart to fail."

"I'm so sorry to hear about that. I can't imagine what it must be like to lose a child. I have four of my own and I don't know what I would do if anything happened to any one of them," I console.

"Well, it's something none of us can anticipate happening. It's very tough and you just have to find a way to go, but you never really get over it," Bob explains.

"Do you have any other children?" I ask.

"Yes, we have a daughter and grandchildren now and that has made things a little easier."

Before parting, we talk a little about golf and Bob suggests that I consider trying to attend one of the annual Pirate Old Timers' Golf Outings. "We get a great turn out and have lots of fun. You can get information from Nellie Briles, if you're interested. I think you'd enjoy it," Bob encourages. I walk with him to his car and thank him again for keeping our meeting, in spite of the adverse weather.

BILL VOISELLE **"Old Number Ninety Six"**
Ninety Six, SC
February, 2000

In the days when I was growing up, baseball's traditions were somewhat more structured than today. In the tradition of those days, uniform numbers were assigned to players, coaches, and managers in a systematic manner, based upon their positions. Managers, coaches, and sometimes catchers wore the numbers 1-9. Infielders wore the numbers 10-19, outfielders 20-29, and pitchers 30-49. There were few exceptions to this tradition until years later, when Al Oliver would wear "0", and Carlton Fisk "72". Bill Voiselle was a notable exception to the tradition of the 40s, and I clearly remember his wearing number 96 when he pitched for the Boston Braves in 1948, when baseball broadcasters would refer to him as "Old number 96."

Virginia Voiselle walks out onto the front porch of the Voiselle's small white frame house just as I pull up in front of the house. She has given me driving directions from Greenville and has anticipated, to the minute, my arrival time. She smiles at her accurateness. A young man is just finishing cutting the grass and grass clippings have blown all over the walkway to the front porch.

"I'm sorry about the mess with the grass. I thought he would be done by now. Come on in, I have two ballplayers for you today," she says. "Bill's brother Jim is here. He was with the Philadelphia A's at one time."

Virginia walks me to a small room just off the living room, where Bill and Jim are seated comfortably in easy chairs, almost opposite each other. The room seems to be a former dining room that now serves as a sort of family room. I introduce myself to Jim and Bill, as they remain seated. Bill extends his left hand in greeting. Virginia has told me on the phone that Bill will be happy to sign for me, as best he can, since he has experienced four strokes of varying severity. Realizing that it is Bill's right side that has been affected by the strokes, I wonder how he will manage his signature.

I open the conversation. "Well, Jim, I know pretty much about Bill, but tell me about your baseball experience."

"Oh, I just had 'a cup of coffee', as they say, with the A's. Mr. Mack called me up to pitch some batting practice at the end of the year, one year. Bill here is the real ballplayer," Jim replies.

"Bill, I know you were with the Giants for awhile, but I remember your playing with the Braves in the late '40s. I never understood why you wore the number 96, but now I know," I tell him.

Bill laughs and picks up the lead. "Oh yes. I pitched in two games in the '48 World Series against Cleveland. Spahn didn't have his stuff in Game 2 and I wound up relieving him in the second or third inning and pitched most of the rest of the game. Then I started Game 5, which was the last game, and lost it. That's a strange story. I was pitching well and we were tied late in the game, seventh or eighth inning, I believe. We had the bases loaded and two outs and I was scheduled to be the next hitter. Everyone knew Southworth would pinch-hit for me, but, for some reason, he sent me up there to hit for myself. I grounded out to Joe Gordon to end the inning. The very next inning, Gordon leads off against me and hits a home run that pretty much ended the game and the Series. Those are great memories."

Bill asks what I would like him to sign. Seeing the two bats and a ball, he smiles and says, "Well, I'll do the best that I can. Those look like nice pieces. I don't want to mess them up."

"Don't worry about it," I say. "I'm just happy to have you add your name to them."

Virginia suggests that Bill move into the kitchen, where the table will give him additional support for his disabled right arm and hand. At 6'4" tall, the move to the kitchen is not an easy one for Bill in his present condition, but he makes the change without complaint. Once seated, using his left hand, he carefully positions the sharpie pen I have given him into his partially paralyzed right hand and slowly begins writing on the barrel of one of the bats.

"Just take your time, honey," Virginia encourages.

"You're doing great," I add.

"He's come a long way from nothing," Virginia says to me, a grateful look in her eye.

Bill completes the signings and, on the way back into the family room, stops to point out a series of photographs depicting a fight on the baseball field, which are displayed on one of the walls in the room.

"That's a fight that started between Frankie Gustine and me, when he played for the Pirates. It turned into a 'free for all.' Their pitchers had been throwing at our guys, particularly

Johnny Hopp (a little guy), throughout the series. So, the day I was pitching, Hopp is our leadoff man and Kirby Higbe (Pirate pitcher) drills him in the side with the first pitch. The next time up, Higbe hits Hopp again! Hopp turns to me on the bench and says, 'Are you going to let them do that?' I'll take care of it, I told him."

Bill continues, "Well, I look to see who's coming to bat in their half of the inning. First guy up is Hank Greenberg. He's 6'4" and about 250 pounds. Next, Ralph Kiner, a young, strong power hitter. Then comes Gustine, a veteran of average size. So, guess who gets the retaliatory bean ball? Gustine! And all hell broke loose."

"What about your time with the Giants?" I ask.

"Well, I probably could have run for mayor of New York when I first came up. I won my first 9 games with the Giants. I had a lead in the 10th game, when rain caused a 45 minute delay. Ott sent me back out after the delay and I gave up the tying run and eventually lost the game. Ott told me anytime I had 2 strikes, no balls on the hitter that I was to waste a pitch. I had Johnny Hopp 0-2 and threw a waste pitch high and outside, which Hopp hit to left field for a triple. Ott thought I had violated his instructions and fined me $1,000. After that, I didn't much care about pitching for Mel Ott."

Before I leave, Bill has Virginia show me a team photograph of the 1944 National League All-Star team that was taken in Pittsburgh's Forbes Field. One by one, I try to identify the players. Faces look familiar, names are hard to come by. Bob Elliott. Connie Ryan. Walker Cooper. Bucky Walters. Frank McCormick. Phil Cavaretta. Stan Musial. Ken Raffensburger. Dixie Walker. Rip Sewell. Bill Voiselle. Whitey Kurowski. Bill helps me with several players that I do not recognize and then asks, "Would you like a copy of that picture?"

Naturally, I accept Bill's offer and Virginia produces a Xerox copy of the original, which she rolls up, places in a cardboard tube, and hands to me with a smile.

Thanking Bill, Jim, and Virginia, I gather my things to leave. Virginia walks me outside, thanks me for coming, and apologizes again for the grass clippings that are still on the sidewalk.

In June 2004, over four years after I had originally visited the Voiselles, I called Virginia to ask if I might be able to get a photographic reprint of the actual photo, for which she had given me a Xerox copy, of the 1944 National League All-Star team to include in my book. She said she would be happy to do so if I would send her a self-addressed mailing envelope, which I did. I also included some money to pay for the reprint. Two weeks later I received the photo, as promised, as well as the money I had sent her for the picture.

AL DARK
Easley, SC
February, 2000

Al is one of those consummate southern gentlemen. Pleasantly soft spoken, he sounds almost anxious to meet me when I finally reach him on the phone late in the afternoon. My morning call had found him on the golf course, according to his wife, who was babysitting 4 grandchildren, 2 of them sick with colds. "Oh, call him back after 4:00 or 4:30. I know he'll want to see you," she had said.

"Sure, come on over. Do you need directions?" Dark says.

Because of the hour, I ask to make sure that I will not be interrupting dinner.

"No, no, just come on over."

It is almost dark when I arrive at the Darks' house, a very attractive single-story ranch-style home on a heavily wooded lot, backing up to a golf course in an upscale residential area. I can see Al through the large picture window of the living room, as I follow the walkway to the front door. He quickly comes to the door, invites me inside, and directs me to take a seat.

"I got your letter," he says. "I remember, because we used to have a catcher named Jack Hiatt and I thought about how similar the names are. Do you have your own pens or shall I get mine," he asks, reaching for one of the bats.

He looks over the signatures on the bats, before signing. "Gee, you have some great stuff here. Davey Williams…my old roommate. Harry Danning…he's a real old-timer."

I invite his attention to Bill Rogell's signature on one of the bats. "Look at this signature. Bill Rogell signed this about a year ago, at age 94."

"Gee! That's amazing. It's hard to believe someone can write that well at 94. Who did he play for? Is he in the Hall of Fame?" Dark asks.

After I tell him about Rogell, Al gets up, walks across the room to a bookcase, and returns with his Baseball Encyclopedia. He looks up Rogell's record and reads some statistics aloud. "He had a pretty decent career. And a long one," Al observes.

"Tell me what it was like, playing for Leo Durocher," I inquire.

"I really liked playing for Leo. I guess it's because we were both strong competitors. Winning was the only thing that mattered to Leo. He didn't have any 'favorites.' A player was just a pawn to him. He treated everyone the same. If you screwed up, it didn't matter who you were, you were going to get chewed out. As long as he felt you were doing your best to help win, you were okay, but he could be murder if he felt you weren't carrying your share of the load."

"Was he a teacher, in any way?" I ask.

"No. Managers didn't really teach. They had their coaches for that, but Leo did influence my managing in one respect. I called all the pitches when I managed. That's because Leo was forever second guessing his catchers, whenever an opponent got a key hit. 'Why did you call THAT pitch? You knew he can hit THAT!' He used to wear Wes Westrum out with his second guessing, so I decided never to let my catchers be in a position to be second guessed."

"Were 1951 and '54 your most memorable seasons?" I query.

"Well, yes, but I'd have to include 1974 in there too. You know, I managed the Oakland A's to the world championship that year! That was definitely a great year. Of course, in '51 we caught the Dodgers and Bobby (Thomson) hit that home run in the playoff. In '54 we swept 4 straight in the Series from a really great Cleveland team. And then that '74 A's season," Al reflects.

I mention having watched Al play many times in old Crosley Field in Cincinnati when I was growing up.

"Oh, that was a great place to play if you were an infielder. That infield was just beautiful, the best in the league. It was a perfect 'turtle back' infield. The ball always stayed down and you never had to worry about a bad hop. That's what made Roy McMillan such a great shortstop. He got to play on the best infield in the league."

I thank Al for allowing me to come by at such a late hour.

"No problem. Thanks for remembering me," he says, sincerely.

Al walks me out through the back of the house. The walls in the hallway from the kitchen to the garage are covered with photos from Al's baseball career. He stops to comment about a photo showing him putting a 'bear hug' from behind on a smiling Joe DiMaggio. Al is wearing a turtle neck and DiMaggio a suit and tie. "You know, that's one of the few times Joe seemed relaxed with me. He was a very difficult person to be around. Quite aloof. I never felt very comfortable around him, but that was one time he sort of let his guard down. That's a very special picture to me."

I tell Al to give Mrs. Dark my regards and thank him again for letting me stop by.

"Anytime, anytime. I've always got time for real baseball fans," is his reply.

ART FOWLER
Spartanburg, SC
February, 2000

I take a calculated risk in driving out to Art's house. I've not been able to get an answer to my several phone calls, but since I seldom have occasion to be in the Carolinas, I decide to take a chance on finding him.

A large sign at the entrance to the driveway says "The Fowlers." A pleasant, but aging ranch style house sits back about 120' from the highway, which has apparently been recently widened into a 4 lane thoroughfare from a 2 lane country road. The Fowlers' driveway is a sweeping semi-circular drive and there are 3 or 4 older model cars displayed at intervals on the lawn next to the driveway, apparently a collection of sorts. A large white car is parked in a finger of the driveway near the house. The front license plate reads "Yankees." This must be the place.

Ruth Fowler, a very pleasant woman, answers the door. When I introduce myself and explain the purpose of my call, she responds, "I'm sorry, but Art has been sick in bed and can't see you, but I'll ask him if he will sign your things. Just a minute, please."

She leaves and walks toward the back of the house, returning in a minute or so to say, "Yes, if you will give me the things you want signed, Art will be glad to sign them for you."

Not wanting to press my luck, I retrieve a single bat and ball from the car and give them to Ruth with a Sharpie pen. "Please, make yourself comfortable and feel free to look around at some of Art's things," she says, as she takes the items I have given her and starts down the hall leading to the bedrooms. There are photos and autographed baseballs everywhere throughout the living room and in a recently remodeled room that apparently was previously a garage or carport. Many of the photos are from Art's days as a player with the Cincinnati Reds in the early '50s. Ruth returns shortly and hands me the signed items.

"What's the matter with Art?" I ask. "I hope it's nothing serious."

"We don't really know. We've been to several different doctors and nobody can tell us what the problem is," she tells me, and then proceeds to explain some of the photos and collectibles that Art has. "You know Art has the catcher's mitt that Thurman Munson used to catch his last game before he was killed in that plane crash. Thurman was going to throw it away, because he had a new one he was going to start using and Art told Thurman he'd like to have it. So, Thurman gave it to him. Some fellow from Florida has been trying to buy that mitt from us for several years now. He's offered us several thousand dollars, but I keep telling him it's not for sale…at ANY price. You know, he would just sell it to someone else for even more money."

I comment about some of the Reds players I recognize in the photos on the wall and tell Ruth about growing up in Cincinnati when Art was pitching there. I mention that my sister-in-law used to babysit for Gus Bell and his wife.

At this point, Ruth expresses some disappointment with the Reds organization. "You know, we really enjoyed Cincinnati. We had some great friends on the team there. But I don't understand the organization. I have a collection that consists of some little items, mostly pins, from each of the teams that Art played or coached with. A few years ago, I wrote to Marge Schott, asking her to send me something from the Reds organization to make our collection complete. Neither she, nor anyone in the Reds organization even bothered answering my letter. I think it's a shame."

As I prepare to leave, Ruth thanks me for coming and apologizes for Art's being too sick to visit personally with me. I leave somewhat saddened, but glad that I took a chance on catching Art. Meeting Ruth Fowler was worth the effort.

Bill & Jack (1951)

BEST WISHES TO
J.W. HEYDE
Frank Crosetti

7/19

J. W.

THE PLAYER END OF ROW IS STUBBY
OVERMIRE, PITCHER. THE PLAYER NEXT TO
BRIDEWESER IS CATCHER GUS NIARHOS –
PLAYER NEAR MANTLE IS PITCHER BOBBY HOGUE –
PLAYER ON TOP ROW I THINK IS PITCHER FRED
SANFORD – HOPE THIS DOES IT FOR YOU –
STILL HOT TO-DAY –

P.S. FORGOT TO GIVE CRO
YOU THIS PICTURE

Dillinger & Mr. Mack

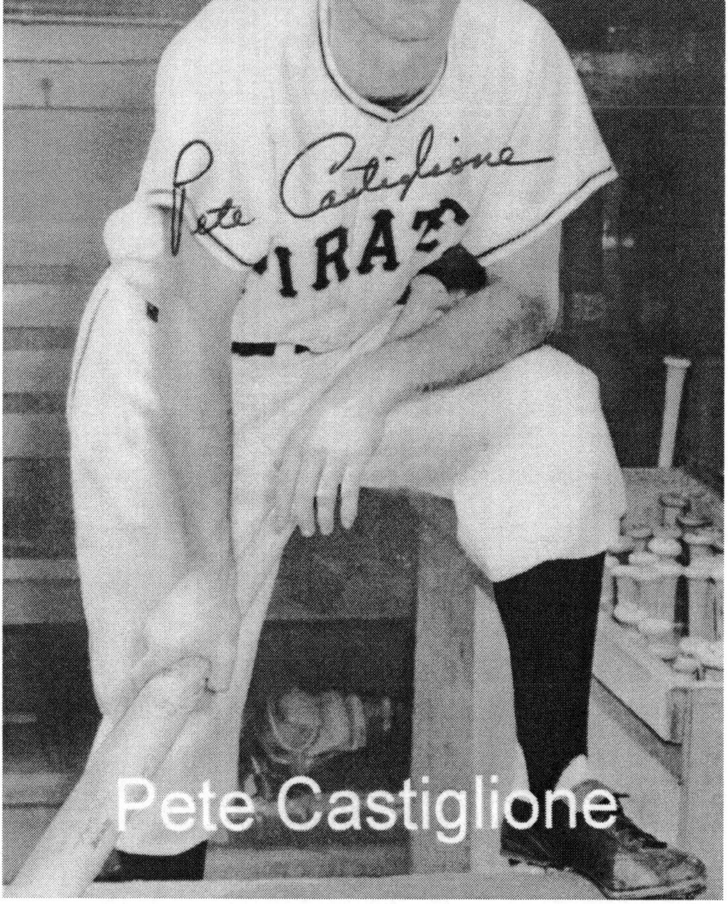
Pete Castiglione
Pete Castiglione

Dino Restelli
1949-51

EW YORK

Grand Reunion, NYC, 2001

Corwin, author, Jansen, G. Spencer

Matt Batts

Carl Erskine

1944 National League All Star Team

VERNON LAW
Provo, UT
April, 2000

Following several unsuccessful attempts to reach Vernon by telephone to arrange a meeting, I take a chance and make the 40 minute drive from Salt Lake City to Provo in hope of finding him home. My trips to Utah are rare, so the decision is made easily.

Fortunately, Vernon, wearing a Pittsburgh Pirates cap and a T-shirt with the number 32 on the back, answers the door and, following my self-introduction, recalls receiving my letter. "You got here just in the nick of time. I just got home and am waiting for a young boy to arrive that I am supposed to work with this afternoon. Let's see what you have for me to sign," he says.

He follows me out to the car and, as I open the trunk to remove my bats, our conversation begins:

"Are you still active with the game?" I inquire.

"Well, my son (former major league infielder Vance Law) coaches the college (BYU) team here and I go over and help him out now and then. And I work with a few of the younger kids in the area," he answers.

"What are your thoughts about baseball these days?"

"The game has changed a lot. Being a pitcher, I particularly notice how pitching and the whole approach to pitching has changed. I guess expansion is the cause for a lot of the differences. You know, when I was playing, a starting pitcher was expected to pitch a complete game. I remember that game I pitched against Milwaukee when the score was tied 0-

0 or 1-1 at the end of 9 innings and Murtaugh was going to take me out. I told him, 'I feel fine, Skip. Just let me go.'"

"After 15 innings we were still tied and again he wanted me to call it an evening. 'I'm okay. I'm getting them 1-2-3 and not throwing that many pitches.' So he keeps me in. Finally, after 18 innings, we're still tied and he tells me I'm through and to go take a shower. Bob Friend takes over in the 19th inning and gives up a run in the top of the 19th to Milwaukee. Then we score 2 in the bottom of the 19th to win. I pitched 18 innings of 1-run ball and get no decision and Friend pitches 1 inning and gets the win! But the kicker is that 3 days later I took my regular turn in Cincinnati against Ewell Blackwell and wound up in another extra inning pitchers duel. Today, pitchers are considered 'good' if they can get through 6 innings."

By this time, Vern has signed the items I have for him and a young boy, looking to be in his early teens, has gotten out of a car driven by his mother and is walking across the lawn toward us, baseball glove in hand. "Well, it looks like my new student has arrived," Vern says. "Sorry I don't have more time, but thanks for stopping by."

The youngster introduces himself to Vern and, as they turn to walk away together, Vernon puts his right arm around the boy's shoulders and starts asking him questions about his pitching.

HERMAN FRANKS
Salt Lake City, UT
April, 2000

The only thing Herman asks when I call to arrange a meeting is "How long will it take?"

Herman lives in a beautiful home on the side of a hill overlooking the Wasatch Valley and Salt Lake City. From the breakfast room, where Herman signs the pieces that I have brought in, the view to the west must cover 25-30 miles. Herman signs willingly, but appears rushed.

"I just got back from San Francisco. The club invited a bunch of us to attend opening day at the new (PacBell) ballpark. It was good to visit with Bobby Thomson and some of the players from our 1950s teams and we all enjoyed having an opportunity to see the new park," Herman explains.

Looking around the house, I don't see a single item that would reflect Herman's long career as a player, coach, manager, and club official in baseball.

"I don't have a bunch of stuff from my baseball days like most of the other fellows have. When I left baseball, I left baseball," Herman states matter of factly. "I'm out of the game now and only occasionally get involved with anything related to baseball."

I take the cue and do not pursue my usual course of asking a few questions to stimulate a recollection of memories or a discussion of the game. Herman thanks me for stopping by, asks where I am going from his home and if I need directions, and walks to the car with me.

While my visit with Herman has been brief, I accomplished my objective of obtaining his autograph…and the view was spectacular!

GRADY HATTON
Warren, TX
August, 2000

Running down Grady Hatton had been a major goal of mine since moving to Texas in 1993. Warren, Texas is not exactly on the beaten path to anywhere, which explains why it took me almost seven years to make the contact. The reason that he was so important to me is that, as a rookie with the Cincinnati Reds in 1946, Grady Hatton was one of the first baseball players that I remember. He wore number 15, played third base, and hit third in the batting order of a mediocre post WWII Reds team. He had been one of my first "favorite" ballplayers.

Having given me directions from downtown Houston to his home in the southeast Texas countryside, and estimated the travel time almost exactly (2 hours), Grady is standing next to his pickup truck, awaiting my arrival. His farmhouse sits well back from the road, at the end of a long driveway. He is wearing his work clothes, a worn denim shirt and overalls. He is stocky, well tanned, and has a very full head of graying hair, combed straight back. He is grinning slightly as I get out of the car.

"Man, this is a long way from Cincinnati," I say, shaking Grady's outstretched hand.

"Yes, I bought this land with the first bonus check I got for signing with the Reds back in the forties. That's a long time ago. It was originally 153 acres, but I've sold off some of it in recent years," he responds. "Bring your stuff inside. It's a lot more comfortable in there and we can sit down. Would you like a Coke? I've got some in the refrigerator."

We sit at a table just off the kitchen. As Grady signs the bats and ball that I have brought in, we talk some baseball.

"How did you like playing in Cincinnati?" I ask.

Grady warms to the question. "Cincinnati was a great place to play. They had great fans, excellent sportswriters, and a nice ballpark. I was lucky to have played in two great baseball cities, with the Reds and (Boston) Red Sox. They were a lot alike as baseball towns, although the attendance in Boston was quite a bit better."

"Those Reds teams you played on were not particularly strong at that time," I remind him.

"Well, that's true. They were just coming off those championship years in '39 and '40. We still had Bucky Walters, Joe Beggs, Johnny Vander Meer, Frank McCormick, and Lonnie Frey, but their best years were behind them. Of course, Ewell Blackwell was always good for drawing a crowd. And Crosley Field had the best infield to play on in the major leagues. Matty Schwab was the groundskeeper and he was the best. The grass was cut at a perfect length all the time and you could shoot pool on the skinned portion of the infield. Never a 'bad hop' on Matty's infield! In Pittsburgh (Forbes Field), the infield had 2 inches of sand on it. In Brooklyn (Ebbetts Field), they cut the grass high and watered the hell out of it. You couldn't hit a ground ball through that infield. In St. Louis (Sportsman's Park), the heat killed all the grass in the infield. So playing in Cincinnati was pretty nice."

"Remember Waite Hoyt (Reds radio broadcaster when Hatton was playing)?" I ask.

"Oh, yes. He used to use that phrase, 'Hatton battin'," Grady recalls.

"You spent some time in the Houston organization when you stopped playing, didn't you?" I continue.

"Yes, I spent many years in various jobs with the Houston club and finished up with a few years in the Giants (San Francisco) organization, working for Bob Lurie. He was a wonderful man and a very good owner. I finished with baseball in 1991. I just got tired of seeing all the money being spent on ballplayers who don't really know how to play the game. They can't bunt! They won't hit behind the runner! They throw to the wrong base! I called Al Rosen, who was the Giants general manager, and said 'Al, I've had enough! Forty-six years in baseball is enough.' You know, he said to me, 'Grady, I don't blame you. I'm getting out myself next year.' And he did."

"You coached for Leo Durocher for awhile. What was Leo like?" I inquire.

"Leo was alright. He always surrounded himself with good baseball men and Leo always kinda' liked me. When I played at Cincinnati, Leo managed the Dodgers, and later the Giants. In those days, it was common for the manager to coach at third base. Leo was the kind of guy who would do anything to win and he used to call me every name in the book when he was in the coach's box at third. I'd just look at him and say 'Go on back in the dugout and get some perfume. I can smell you all the way over here.' I think he liked the fact that he couldn't get me riled up."

Not noticing any baseball items on display, I mention my observation to Grady.

"I didn't keep much. I used to have a pretty good assortment of team autographed baseballs, but I gave most of them to the local kids around here to play with. They didn't have any decent balls to use. The rest I gave to my son, who lives next door, but I really don't know what he's done with them."

Having enjoyed my long awaited meeting with Grady, I thank him for his time, wish him well, and get directions for the best route for my return trip to Dallas. As I drive out the driveway, I see Grady, waving good-bye in my rear view mirror.

PETE SUDER
Aliquippa, PA
October, 2000

"Well, my wife's in the hospital, but if you're in the area, come on over."

Pete meets me on his front porch and takes me inside the house, into the kitchen. I decline his offer of a Coca-Cola and thank him for letting me stop by. Pete is slender, wears thick glasses, and is quite talkative. He shows me some items that he has just received in the mail to sign.

"Look at this! This guy says he has 800 single signed balls in his collection! He sent this Swiss Army knife to me for signing a ball. Man, the guy must have spent a fortune getting all those autographs," Pete observes.

Pete doesn't waste any time letting me know what he thinks of present day ballplayers. "I don't think there's a ballplayer alive worth $1,000,000. Jason Kendall says he'll stay in Pittsburgh if they'll give him a six year contract for $60,000,000! How ridiculous is that? When I came up in 1941, I got $4,500 for the season and we got paid $8 a day for meals when we were on the road. I do think the players of today, as a group, are a lot faster and stronger though. I mean I've seen guys hit the ball out of the park with a shattered bat! But they aren't very smart. You know, Mike Piazza lost that game the other night. (Pete is referring to Game 5, the deciding game, of the 2000 World Series, which had been played 2 days earlier.) If he had taken that throw (from center-fielder Jay Payton) in front of home plate, where he should have been, he would have had him, but he was behind the plate and allowed the ball to hit the runner and let 2 runs score. That was a terrible play for a guy making the kind of money he does!"

Pete reminds me that the infield he played on with the Philadelphia A's still holds the single season record for most double plays. Hank Majeski, Eddie Joost, and Ferris Fain completed the infield with Suder, who played second base. "You know, I was never taken out by a baserunner when I was turning a double play. Majeski and Joost always gave me the ball right here (he holds his hands out in front of his chest) and I knew how to cheat on the pivot. We were a hell of an infield!"

Pete credits Jimmy Dykes for helping him become a better hitter. "When I came up, I was a pretty free swinger. Dykes pulled me aside one day and said, 'Pete, if you'd stop swinging for the fences, you'd add 50 points to your batting average.' Well, I took his advice and by the All-Star break I was hitting .324 and I had been a .250-.260 hitter!"

As most former A's players, Pete speaks very respectfully of Connie Mack, his manager for several years. "Mr. Mack was a wonderful man, but he was extremely conservative and, in his later years wasn't really in touch with the game. He always was looking for the base on balls. He wouldn't think of giving even his best hitters the 'hit' sign on a 3-1 or 3-0 count. The last year or so he would even fall asleep on the bench during the game. And he was always tight with the payroll."

I ask Pete which pitchers he hit best and which he had trouble with.

"Vic Raschi of the Yankees was always tough on me. I think he must have invented the slider. He'd throw what looked like a fastball right in the heart of the strike zone and if I got my bat on it at all, it was right on the end of the bat. I used a 35-inch bat and one day Al Simmons (an A's coach) told me to try his 40-inch bat, which he kept in our bat rack. With that bat, I was finally able to hit some of Raschi's pitches to rightfield. I had my best luck against Mel Parnell and Maury McDermott of the Red Sox and Bob Feller. Matter of fact, I understand that Feller once said that the three toughest hitters he faced were Joe DiMaggio, Ted Williams, and Pete Suder. That's pretty exclusive company."

In answer to another question, Pete states that he feels Joe DiMaggio is the greatest ballplayer he ever saw and that Ted Williams was the best hitter. "I came out of the batting cage one day during batting practice before a game in Fenway Park and Ted Williams called me aside and said, 'Pete, you're not watching the ball come off your bat. You're swinging here and your eyes are focused here.' I was really surprised that he did that, because I didn't really know him and he played for an opposing team, but he was just a fanatic about hitting."

As Pete looks over the signatures on the bats I have brought for him to sign, he comments about several of the players that he played with and asks me about how some of them are doing. When he is finished, I thank him for letting me come by, extend my best wishes to him and his wife, and take my leave.

BOB KUZAVA
Wyandotte, MI
November, 2000

I arrive at McDonald's in Wyandotte at about 9:10 AM, 10 minutes later than our agreed meeting time. A heavy set older gentleman, cane in hand, notices me, looking around the restaurant.

"Are you looking for Bob?" he says. "He said to have you come to the house. He was expecting a call from his wife and had to go back home." He directs me to Bob's home, which is just a short distance away. I thank him and leave for Bob's house.

Bob's wife is in a local hospital undergoing some stress tests, having experienced chest pains two days earlier. Bob has agreed to meet with me in spite of this circumstance. He had told me that her test would not be completed until mid-day and he would be available until he heard from her.

Answering the door at his home, Bob looks very much like the photos I have seen of him during his playing days in the '50s. He is trim and his silver hair is still worn in the brush cut style of the '50s. He welcomes me with a smile. "You must be Jack. I'm sorry I couldn't wait longer, but I'm glad you got my message and found me. Why don't you get your bats and bring them on inside. We can use the kitchen."

As he signs the items I have brought in, Bob talks about his experiences as a major league pitcher. "I was fortunate to play on three Yankees world championship teams and to have pitched in the '51 and '52 World Series. In the '52 Series, Casey (Stengel) brought me in in the seventh inning of the seventh game against the Dodgers in Ebbetts Field. The bases were loaded with one out and Snider was the hitter. I had always had pretty good success against Snider and when I got him out I figured my job was done, as Jackie Robinson was the next hitter and I figured Stengel would use a right-hander to pitch to Jackie. When he came out to the mound, he just said to me 'Go get 'em!' Robinson hit a little pop-up in the infield, but Joe Collins (first baseman) lost the ball in the sun and Billy Martin had to sprint in and catch the ball around his knees at the last minute to save Collins and the game. I finished that game and we wound up winning it and the Series."

"You must have been happy to be playing with the Yankees after having been with the Washington Senators for several years," I remark.

"Well, it was a nice experience, but I was quite happy with the Senators, because I was the 'Ace' of the pitching staff there and Bucky Harris was a great manager to play for. When I was with the Yankees, I was just an occasional reliever and 'spot' starter."

"What did you think of Ted Williams?" I ask.

"Ted was the best hitter the game has ever seen. Just think about it. He hit .406 in 1941. That would be the equivalent of hitting about .425 today, because in '41 hitters did not get the benefit of the 'sacrifice fly' rule. In those days they were charged with a time at bat if a fly ball advanced a baserunner. And he was hitting against a lot better pitching than you see these days. Then there's the fact that he spent probably the four best years of his life in the service. He was simply the best and he really worked at hitting. No matter what team I was playing for, whenever we played the Red Sox and Williams was taking batting practice, everyone stopped whatever they were doing and watched Ted hit. There have been some good hitters since, but the only hitters that I have seen that really 'worked' at hitting are George Brett and Tony Gwynn."

"What about DiMaggio?" I continue.

"He was a wonderful player. When I got to the Yankees in '51 he was just a shadow of the player he had been. I think he should have won the MVP in '41 when he had that hitting streak, but the sportswriters didn't like the way Joe treated them and voted for Williams instead. I think DiMaggio got a 'bum wrap' from the sportswriters. He was always nice to people whenever I saw him and he was always nice to me."

"How did you get started in baseball?"

"I was playing high school baseball right here in Wyandotte. One summer I signed to play Class D ball at Mansfield, Ohio. I went 4 and 7 (4 wins, 7 losses) that year. The next year I played at Charleston, West Virginia with Don Newcombe, Red Embree, Cliff Mapes, and a bunch of other future major leaguers and went 23-2. I wound up getting started in the Cleveland organization, but played for the Senators, White Sox, and Yankees, as well as spending several years in the service during the '40s in North Africa, Burma, and some other spots."

"What do you think of major league baseball today?" I ask.

"It's not the same," Bob says. "No ballplayer is worth a million dollars a year. I spent 16 years as a player and another 10 years coaching and scouting and made less than $300,000 in my entire baseball career. I was being paid $9,000.00 as a scout for Charlie Finley my last year. I was on the road all summer, away from my wife and children, and told Finley I needed a raise if I was to continue. He said, 'Well, that's all we have budgeted. I can't help you.' Then a couple of weeks later I read that he had spent $30,000.00 on a party for the press and media, so I called and asked him about that. His reply was 'Well, we have to do those things now and then.' So I quit and went to work driving a beer truck for one of my neighbors making $30,000.00 a year and I didn't have to be away from home and my family. As you can see, we don't have anything real fancy here, but it's all we need and we're quite happy," Bob says.

GEORGE SPENCER
Galena, OH
November, 2000

It's just after noon on a dull and rainy Saturday when George welcomes me into his home in a wooded Columbus suburb and introduces me to his wife, Billie. The three of us sit down at the dining room table and, somehow, we get started talking about George's old New York Giants team mates…where they are and how they are doing. George and Billie are particularly interested in Davey and Sue Williams, whom they had been in regular contact with but have not heard from recently. Since Davey lives in a Dallas suburb, I tell them that I will call him and pass on their "greetings" when I return to Dallas. They are surprised to learn from me that Ray Katt has recently passed away.The conversation continues through Montia Kennedy, Ray Noble, Wes Westrum, Clint Hartung, Larry Jansen, and others. George and Billie share remembrances as each player is mentioned.

George tells a story about Ray Noble. "Noble (pronounced 'NO-blay') was a very husky catcher, but he would fool you with his speed. He was faster than many of his Giants teammates. One day Eddie Stanky baited him. 'Hey Ray! I'll race you, home to first, for $10.' Somebody started them and Noble took off like a shot and Stanky just sort of jogged down to first base. Noble was grinning from ear to ear when Stanky said 'Well, give me my ten bucks.' Noble says 'What do you mean? I beat you by fifteen yards!' Stanky says 'I know, but I said I'd race you. I didn't say I'd beat you.'"

He shares his thoughts on some other ballplayers of his era. "Willie Mays could do something I've never seen another outfielder do. He could consistently make the throw from anywhere in center field to home plate perfectly on one bounce. His ball would hit the infield near second base and carry, on one bounce, all the way to the plate. He threw straight over the top and had so much backspin on the ball that it had this tremendous 'skip' when it hit the ground. And he got rid of the ball faster than any outfielder I have seen. Of course, you couldn't tell him anything. He used to always throw on the fly to third base, which meant the cutoff man could not make another play, if it was appropriate. One day I said to Willie, 'You know, if you would make that throw lower the cutoff man might be able to do something with it.' He just scowled at me and said, 'Who are you now, COACH Spencer???' "

George says he thinks that Jackie Robinson got too much credit as the man who broke the color line in baseball. He considers Branch Rickey the one deserving the credit. He does, however, have the greatest respect for Robinson as a ballplayer. "He was the fiercest competitor that I have ever seen. He could beat you so many different ways and he had an incredible intensity on the field."

Clint Hartung is the subject of another one of George's stories. "Clint was a great big guy (6'4"), but he could run like a deer. He fooled a lot of folks, because he was so big and they didn't think he could be very fast. One day in spring training we were playing the Cleveland Indians and Al Rosen was playing third base. Hartung hit a routine ground ball to third and Rosen fielded it cleanly, took his time gripping the ball in his glove, and made a good throw to first, but Hartung was already a step and a half past the bag when the throw got there. We were in the third base dugout and we really let Rosen have it. 'That's right Al, take your time.' 'Get those seams right Al, no hurry.' He really got an ear full."

Realizing that a fog is beginning to augment the light rain that has been falling, and facing a 1½ hour drive back to Dayton, where I am spending the Thanksgiving holiday, I thank George and Billie for their time and hospitality. I promise to call Davey Williams when I get back to Dallas, to pass along the Spencers' greetings. George and Billie walk me out to the driveway and assure me that I am welcome to return for another visit anytime I happen to be in the area.

JACK HARSHMAN
San Diego, CA
December, 2000

The house at 2227 Commonwealth Avenue, in an older section on the northeast side of downtown San Diego, is a well kept home with a wrought iron fence running along the sidewalk in front of it. It is a two story house with two heavily laden citrus trees in the front yard. While modest, it is clearly the most impressive home in an otherwise ordinary 1940s-era neighborhood. A sign on the fence, near the front gate, reads: "SOLD".

The front door is open and a small barking terrier responds to my knocking on the screen door. A moment later, Jack Harshman appears. "Hi, Jack. I'll bet that dog really scares you. Come on in. He'll be climbing in your lap in about two seconds. Let's go upstairs."

Jack directs me upstairs to a large TV room on the second floor and offers me a seat on the sofa. He takes a chair across the room, facing me. The New Orleans Saints – St. Louis Rams playoff game is on TV. A plastic grocery bag full of orange colored fruit, tied at the top, is sitting on a coffee table next to me, at the end of the couch. Jack points to the bag, saying "Those are some tangerines from the trees out front. I thought you might like to take them with you.

They're really sweet and there's not a seed in them. Could I offer you something to drink…a Coke or something?"

I ask for a glass of ice water and Jack returns with two glasses. One is an 8 ounce glass of ice water, the other a smaller glass of orange and tangerine juice. "Here, try this. It's from right out of the yard. The oranges are a week or so from being ready and they're a little tart, but the tangerines' sweetness balances it out." The drink is unmistakably fresh, but on the bitter side. I thank him and follow the juice with some water. The dog is nuzzling my hand, wanting to be petted. I oblige.

Jack is quite relaxed and easy to talk with. He remarks about the fact that when he went to the big leagues in the early '50s, major league baseball did not have a presence on the west coast. (St. Louis was the western-most city with a major league franchise until Walter O'Malley and Horace Stoneham moved the Brooklyn Dodgers and New York Giants to Los Angeles and San Francisco respectively in 1958.) As a result, his performances in New York and Chicago, as well as some activity with Minneapolis and Nashville minor league teams, went pretty much unnoticed by people in his own hometown of San Diego. Even today, he explains, he is seldom recognized as a former big-leaguer by people in the San Diego area, except when he is playing golf with Bob Skinner, another San Diegan and former Pittsburgh Pirate, who is better known. He hands me a folded and faded newspaper clipping from The Sporting News, dated September 19, 1951. "I thought you might be interested in reading this," he says. "It kinda' explains why I became a pitcher."

It reads: *Jack Harshman, Nashville Vol first baseman, recorded two slugging feats this season that may be unprecedented. Although batting only .251 for the season, Harshman hit 47 home runs and he also knocked in more runs (141) than the number of hits he collected (136). The 23-year-old lefthanded swatter led the league in homers and also total bases with 303. He established an all-time Southern Association record on the final day of the season, September 9, when he smashed his sixth home run with the bases full, one over Carl Sawatski's previous mark set with Nashville in 1949.*

Jack explained that his inability to hit for average prompted him to make the switch to pitching. Leo Durocher's attempt to install Harshman as the starting first-baseman with the New York Giants had not been successful and had led to Jack's assignment to Nashville. "You know, the New York sportswriters can be brutal when they don't like the way things are going. They really got nasty with Durocher for continuing to play me when I was not hitting. He just had to make a change. When I came back to the Giants a few years later as a pitcher, I did pretty well, but Leo had fallen in love with Alan Worthington. So I was eventually let go and wound up with the White Sox and had a respectable career as a left-handed pitcher."

Somehow the conversation turns to catchers and Jack talks about Wes Westrum and Sal Yvars, who were with the Giants when he was with New York. "Yvars was sort of a wild man, unpredictable. You never knew what he was going to do. A pretty decent hitter, but he had the misfortune of playing on a team that had Wes Westrum. Wes was a very good catcher and he was about as physically tough as they come. I remember a game in the minors when he fielded a pitch in the dirt and the ball hit his bare hand in such a way so as to tear the webbing between two of his fingers, just split it open! That sort of injury would put a lot of catchers out of action for several games, but not Westrum. He didn't even leave the game. He was one tough 'cookie.'"

We conclude our visit and I take the article Jack has offered me, the bag of tangerines, and head downstairs to the car. I thank him again for the fruit, assure him that I will return the original press clipping, and wish him the best with his pending move.

ED ERAUTT
San Diego, CA
December, 2000

Ed answers the door at his small home on the east side of San Diego. I immediately recognize him by his crew cut hair, which was common with many of the players in the 40s and '50s. I remember him as a second-line starting pitcher with the Reds when I was growing up in Cincinnati. He invites me into the living room, where he introduces me to his wife and two of his grandsons and one of their friends, who are playing video games on the TV.

Ed doesn't have a lot to say, but he asks me about many of his former teammates, John Pramesa, Johnny Wyrostek, Frank Baumholtz, Claude Corbett, Ray Lamanno, and others. He seems surprised to learn that many of them have passed away. He has not kept track of them. I fill him in on some of the players I have visited, like Grady Hatton and Ken Raffensberger.

Ed picks up on my mention of Raffensberger, a knuckle-balling left-handed pitcher with the Reds in the early '50s. "I remember how 'Raffy" used to always go over how he was going to pitch to the hitters before a game. Whenever we played the Cardinals he'd always say, 'I'm going to pitch Musial outside and try to hold him to doubles.' Funny thing is that Raffensberger probably had better luck pitching to Musial than any other pitcher in the league. He used to drive Stan nuts with all the 'junk.'"

We talk a little about Ewell Blackwell and how close he came, in 1947, to duplicating Johnny Vander Meer's back-to-back no-hitters. "He (Blackwell) was one of the best pitchers of his day. Hitters hated to bat against him and he knew it, and took advantage of it. He'd have had that second no-hitter if it hadn't been for Eddie Stanky's scratch hit with one out in the ninth. (I remember the game well, from my childhood.) Stanky turned out to be the guy who let me go from the Cardinals at the end of my career. He and I never did get along."

Before I leave, Ed shows me a large photo of himself in a Cincinnati uniform that hangs on the wall in his dining room. I recognize it as an enlargement of a 5X7 photo that Mabley & Carew, a Cincinnati department store, used to give away as a promotional item to Reds fans in the '50s. It is a photo that I had as part of a childhood collection.

I thank Ed for his time and mention that I may want to stop back and have him autograph another item on a future visit to San Diego. He says I am welcome any time.

PAUL GIEL
Minnetonka, MN
March, 2001

My memory of Paul Giel goes back to the early 1950s, when I was in junior high school becoming interested in football. At that time, Paul Giel was making a reputation as an All-American halfback on the University of Minnesota football team. As my meeting with Paul would reveal, he went on to a career of incredible versatility that crossed the lines of many sports and types of activities.

When I called Paul in 2000 to try to arrange a meeting during a brief business trip I was making into the Minneapolis area, he was receptive but was unable to accommodate me, due to a commitment to a fund raising golf tournament sponsored by the Heart Institute. My call this year would have met a similar fate had it not been for the graciousness and generosity of Paul Giel.

"Well, I'm catching a plane to Naples, Florida early Thursday morning to attend a Heart Institute seminar being conducted for some Minnesota retirees living down there, but if you call me when you get settled in your hotel Wednesday evening, maybe I can stop by and visit for a few minutes."

Despite my offer to go to his home or meet him somewhere between his home and my hotel, Paul delayed his dinner and packing and walked into the lobby of the Wyndham hotel, where we agreed to meet, at 7:30 PM. Wearing a business suit and tie and being somewhat shorter than I had expected, Paul presented a rather distinguished appearance. Recognizing the bats by my chair in the lobby, he said, "You must be Jack. I'm Paul Giel."

After thanking him for coming, I inquired about his involvement with the Heart Institute. "Well, you know, I had heart problems and some bypass surgery several years ago and for the past few years I've been quite active and involved with the Heart Institute," Paul explained.

I mention my memory of him as a football player at Minnesota and Paul picks up the story. "Yes, in 1951 I was a 'backup' quarterback and Wes Fesler was the coach. One of our halfbacks got into trouble with Fesler for skipping classes, or some such thing, and Fesler threw him off the team and moved me into his spot. I started and played left-halfback the rest of my time there. Then, fortunately, I wound up going into professional baseball. I joined the New York Giants in 1954 and was on the world championship team there, when Willie Mays made that great catch. I came home from two years in the service in 1960 and was sent to Pittsburgh, which was the year they won the championship. Then Mr. Griffith asked me to come back here with the Twins in 1961. When they sent me to Kansas City, I knew it was time to call it quits."

"About that time, the University (Minnesota) called and offered me a position in the athletic department and I spent 17 years as athletic director, until they decided to get rid of me. Then I took a broadcasting job with the Twins and, when the North Stars (ice hockey team) came to Minnesota, I spent a couple of years working for Lou Nanny doing public relations work. So, I've had a great life doing all sorts of things in sports."

As he looks over the autographs on my New York Giants bat, Paul's memory is stimulated. "Geez,... Larry Jansen! I remember when I was a kid, my dad worked for the railroad. One time he took me on the train down to Chicago to see a Cubs game against the Giants. Larry Jansen was pitching for the Giants against Johnny Schmitz. Walker Cooper was the Giants catcher. What a thrill it was to see those guys play in Wrigley Field. And then to wind up playing on the same team with Larry Jansen when I went to the Giants was like having a dream come true. Alvin Dark...what a leader! Al was about the only player that Leo Durocher didn't mess around with. I think it was because he recognized and respected Al's leadership and Al always gave the game everything he had. Davey Williams...hated to fly. Davey always said that if the Lord had wanted man to fly he would have given him feathers. George Spencer...an old Ohio State pitcher."

Paul finishes signing a ball and stands up to leave. "I'd love to stay and talk for awhile, but my wife is waiting dinner for me and we have to pack for our trip tomorrow."

I thank Paul for going out of his way for me and wish him a pleasant trip to Florida. I also decide to include a contribution to the Heart Institute in my "thank you" note to him.

Paul Giel died of a heart attack on May 23, 2002, while driving to watch his grandson play baseball.

AL CORWIN
LARRY JANSEN
GEORGE SPENCER
Uniondale, NY
March, 2001

"The Grand Reunion," celebrating the 50th anniversary of the 1951 baseball season, was held in New York the last weekend in March. The festivities, honoring the Brooklyn Dodgers, New York Giants, and New York Yankees, and focusing on Bobby Thomson's "Shot Heard 'Round The World" in the 1951 National League Playoff series, included a banquet at the Marriott Marquis Hotel in Manhattan on Friday night, followed by an autograph show, with approximately 50 players from the three 1951 New York area teams, at a Long Island community center, on Saturday and Sunday. While staying at the Marriott Uniondale Hotel on Long Island, I had the opportunity to visit informally with many of the ballplayers who were participating in the weekend activities and also staying at the hotel. Having become personal friends with George and Billie Spencer, the result of my visit with them at their home in Columbus, OH the previous November, I was invited to join their group for dinner at the hotel on Saturday night. The table talk was, not surprisingly, about baseball.

Appreciative of being invited to join this group for dinner, I buy a round of cocktails before the meal. Larry Jansen and I order vodka and tonic. The others are happy with iced tea or a soft drink. It doesn't take long for the conversation to roll around to the storied rivalry between the Giants and the Dodgers. I ask the group, all former New York Giants players, about the true nature of the rivalry and whether there was, in fact, any "bad blood" between the teams during the 1950s.

Al Corwin starts, "I think it was just a very intense and competitive rivalry between two good New York teams. I know that, for me, there was absolutely nothing like going into Ebetts Field in Brooklyn to play a series against the Dodgers. I mean that stadium just had a special aura when the Giants and Dodgers played. The stands were so close to the field and the fans were so close to the players. There was just a feeling of excitement anytime we went in there and, of course, we were usually competing strongly with them for a pennant."

Larry Jansen, a top Giants pitcher in those days, chimes in, "Al's right, but I didn't much care for Ebetts Field. I didn't pitch well there. The short left field wall was always a problem for me with that predominantly right-hand hitting Brooklyn lineup. I guess that's why I usually wasn't selected to pitch when we went in there. Leo would hold me out for the next opponent, usually Boston or Philadelphia. Then, of course, we had Stanky and Durocher on our side. They both sort of felt that they had been run out of Brooklyn and didn't miss a chance to stir the pot whenever we played the Dodgers."

George Spencer adds another perspective. "All that's true, but you also had some pretty combative personalities in the mix. Jackie (Robinson) was a ferocious competitor and we were always having to deal with him. His running over Davey Williams upset a lot of us and we were always looking for ways to contain Jackie. One weapon we had was

Sal Maglie. Sal wouldn't back down from anyone and he knew who was vulnerable to "chin music" (pitching hard inside) and who wasn't. He knew that Jackie couldn't be intimidated, but he also knew that Campanella and Furillo could both be intimidated and he 'put them on their ass' at least once every time he pitched against them."

"Yes, there were definitely some personality issues that added fuel to the fire whenever we played against the Dodgers," Jansen comments.

Somehow, "Dusty" Rhoades becomes the topic of conversation and George says, "I don't know if the guy has a nerve in his body. I've never seen anyone so unaffected by anything and everything. Nothing ever bothered him. He just went day-to-day doing his thing, totally relaxed. I think he's still that way. Nobody ever knows where he is. One day he's living in Florida and the next he's at his place in Las Vegas. Easy come, easy go. That's how he was when he pinch hit so well in the '54 World Series and that's the way he is today, wherever he is."

Billie Spencer (George's wife) remembers "Dusty" when he first came up to the Giants. "We were playing a series in Cincinnati and I had a seat near the Giants dugout. Sometime during batting practice this big country boy in street clothes, carrying sort of a carpet bag, comes ambling through the stands down near where I was sitting and asked if I know where the Giants clubhouse was. I told him how to get to the clubhouse and he just sort of stood there, looking around, like he was lost or didn't understand me. I thought for a minute that I was going to have to take him by the hand and lead him to the clubhouse, myself!"

Hoyt Wilhelm becomes another topic of conversation. Wilhelm, a knuckle-ball pitcher, was a key member of the

Giants pitching staff in the '50s and went on to be elected to the baseball Hall of Fame.

"It's hard to believe, but Wilhelm was lucky to make it with the Giants," Corwin observes. "Hoyt came up as a prospective starting pitcher, but he didn't have enough to be a successful big league pitcher until he developed his knuckle-ball. Leo (Durocher) didn't care much for knuckle-ballers and was ready to let him go, but Herman Franks talked him into trying Hoyt out as a relief pitcher. Leo wasn't very excited about the idea, but someone on the staff went on the disabled list, so Leo decided to give Wilhelm a try. The rest is history. And I'll never forget how he used to sit on the dugout steps, rubbing his fingernails across the concrete. He used the concrete to file his nails and those nails were always perfectly straight"

Al Corwin died October 23, 2003.

EDDIE PELLAGRINI
Weymouth, MA
July, 2001

Eddie lives in a large gray traditional New England home in a well maintained section of Weymouth. A high, untrimmed hedge runs along the sidewalk and down the property line, almost hiding the house from view. The only break in the hedge is at the walk that leads to the front door. As I enter the foyer, the dining room is immediately on the right, and the living room is to the left. Both rooms are totally cluttered with old photographs, newspaper clippings, and other memorabilia, lying on tables, chairs, the floor, propped up against table and chair legs, on the mantel, everywhere! I notice an unusual number of photos of Babe Ruth among the items and mention my observation to Eddie.

"Well, my mother loved Babe Ruth and I was always a Yankee fan, even though I grew up in Boston," Eddie comments. He walks across the living room, picks up a plastic photograph protector with an 8 X 10 sepia toned photo of a smiling, young Babe Ruth in a tank top shirt, with his arms folded across his chest. Ruth appears to be in his mid-20s, and the smile on his face is one of delightful 'devilment.' I notice that the photo is an original professional portrait photo. "I'll bet you've never seen that picture of Babe before," Eddie proclaims proudly. "It was given to me by his granddaughter."

He points me toward another picture, a framed 8 X 10, propped up on a table on the other side of the living room. "Can you tell me who everyone is in that picture?" Eddie challenges. I walk across the room, put on my glasses, and easily identify Ted Williams, Pellagrini, John F. Kennedy, and Hank Greenberg. Kennedy appears very young, thin (almost ill), and is wearing a wide lapelled overcoat. The others are in uniform, with Williams and Greenberg each holding a bat and appearing to be talking to one another.

Ed tells the story. "The club used to allow the veterans' groups to bring their people into some of the games and they usually seated them somewhere behind home plate. On that day, one of the press photographers approached me during batting practice about having my picture taken with some fellow. I assumed he was with one of the veterans' groups and agreed. As the photographer was setting up to shoot the picture, Willams and Greenberg were standing close by talking about hitting, so I grabbed them and brought them into the picture as well. After the photo was taken and Kennedy, whom none of us knew at the time, had gone back to his seat, the photographer said to me. 'You know, that guy's going to run for congress and he didn't really want Williams and Greenberg in the picture. He just wanted a picture with you that he could show to people in the predominantly Italian voting districts!'"

"Many years later, when Kennedy was President and Williams was managing the Washington Senators, the Senators came to town for a game with the Red Sox and Ted called me and invited me out to the game. After the game, one of the Red Sox publicity people came up to Ted and told him that President Kennedy was going to be at the next day's game and wanted to know if they could get a picture of him (Ted) with President Kennedy. Well, Ted didn't much care for Kennedy and told the guy in no uncertain terms that he would <u>NEVER</u> have his picture taken with 'that *#@% s.o.b.' After the guy left, I said, 'You know, Ted, I've got a picture of you with Kennedy.' He looked at me and said, 'You're full of shit, Pelly!' So the next time I saw Ted I showed him that picture and he couldn't believe it and was mad as hell about it."

"How would you compare Ted Williams with Joe DiMaggio?" I ask.

"Well, first of all, I played with Ted and am a good friend of his. He was easily the best hitter I ever saw, but DiMaggio was the best all-around baseball player I ever saw. DiMaggio could do everything well and could beat you with his bat, his arm, his legs, his mind. Ted was just one hell of a hitter. Beyond that, he was pretty ordinary," Ed answers.

Ed is not one who lacks opinion, especially about baseball matters, so I step out on a limb. "What are your thoughts about the Pete Rose situation?" I inquire.

Pellagrini snaps back, "I wouldn't let him in the Hall of Fame! He gambled on baseball and that's the cardinal sin, but I think they've got a lot of other stuff on him too. I've met Pete and he was quite likeable. Nobody can deny he was a hell of a ballplayer, but I wouldn't let him in."

Ed talks about his playing days with the Red Sox, Phillies, Browns, Reds, and Pirates, as well as his 31 years as coach of the Boston College baseball team after he left the big leagues. Although he grew up in Boston, he says he would have preferred to have spent his career in Philadelphia, with the Phillies, where he says he enjoyed playing the most.

Before I leave, Ed tells me that if I am ever interested in attending a Red Sox fantasy camp in Florida, he will be glad to get me a "special deal," as he works the camps and thinks I would enjoy attending.

BILL WERBER
Horsham, PA
October, 2001

My long quest to meet Bill Werber has ended successfully. It has been at least a three year effort and the reward was worth the wait! As one of the few remaining living members of the 1940 World Champion Cincinnati Reds, Werber has been a person I desperately wanted to meet. I first contacted him by mail in 1998, when he was living in Florida. An answer to my letter came back saying that he would be glad to meet me and sign a few items, but he had recently relocated to Charlotte, NC and I would have to reach him there. It wasn't until early 2000 that my travels took me to North Carolina and, when I called to make arrangements to visit Bill, the timing couldn't have been worse. In his early 90s, life seemed to be catching up with Bill Werber.

"Jack, I'm sorry, but I'm just not up to seeing anyone right now. My wife is in the hospital dying and I've just lost a leg to diabetes. It's just not a good time. Maybe sometime later."

The conversation was short, but friendly. I wished him well and hoped for a future opportunity.

The opportunity presented itself quite unexpectedly, when I learned that Bill would be attending the 8th Annual Fall Reunion of the Philadelphia A's Historical Society in Horsham, PA. I had previously attended some of the Society's events and they had always been enjoyable, with many former ballplayers attending. I wasted no time in making plans to attend.

Bill Werber and Dominic DiMaggio were the featured speakers at the Society's Sunday breakfast and autograph show. Although Bill was quite busy, I had a chance to introduce myself, remind him of our previous correspondence and conversation, talk a little bit about Cincinnati, and meet 2 of his sons. At 93, Bill Werber is healthy (except for his diabetes), alert, articulate, extremely personable, and displays a quick and delightful sense of humor. He displayed all of these traits in the course of his address to the group and in his personal interaction with people attending the event. His stories reflect memories of his baseball playing days.

"Connie Mack was the quintessential baseball manager. There was never another like him. A testament to Mr. Mack, not so much as a manager, but as a man, was the fact that he would never correct a ballplayer in front of another ballplayer. Now, don't misunderstand. Mr. Mack knew baseball and he knew how he wanted things done, but he also knew that people make mistakes. So, although he never corrected someone in front of his fellow players, Mr. Mack did not overlook a ballplayer's mistakes. If a player happened to 'goof up' a play during the course of a game, it was not unusual for that player to be 'invited' to Mr. Mack's office by the clubhouse attendant before the following day's game. Mr. Mack would take that opportunity to review for the player what he had done incorrectly, then explain how he would like to have had the situation handled. He would then request that, should a similar situation present itself in the future, the ballplayer would handle it Mr. Mack's way."

Knowing that Eddie Joost, a teammate on the 1940 Cincinnati Reds team, was in the audience, Werber took the opportunity to relate an object lesson. "You know, in 1940, when our team was fighting to get into the World Series, we ran into a streak of bum luck late in the season. In August, our backup catcher, Willard Hershberger, slit his wrists and bled to death in the Copley Plaza Hotel in Boston. Then a little later, an iron lid on an ice chest in the dugout slid off a big block of ice and landed on our second baseman's (Lonnie Frey) toe. Not long after that, Ernie Lombardi, our catcher, sustained an ankle injury that ended his season. Things were not going very well for us at that point. Now, we happened to have a young utility infielder who thought pretty highly of his own abilities. He thought he was a better third baseman than I, and he probably was. He also thought that he was a better shortstop than Billy Myers, and he may have been. And he doubtless thought he was a better second baseman than Lonnie Frey, although Lonnie was one of the best. But the point was, a ballplayer isn't paid to make such assessments. That's the manager's job and Bill McKechnie didn't see things the same way as his young utility player. But, as fate would have it, that young player got his opportunity to play as Lonnie Frey's replacement in the 1940 World Series and Eddie Joost contributed significantly, with solid defensive play and some key hits, to help us win the World Series in 1940. I know you're here somewhere. Eddie Joost, please stand up."

Bill Werber was a hustling ballplayer and he had very good speed. He tells the following story about Jimmy Foxx. "When I was with the A's, Jimmy Foxx was on the team. As you know, Jimmy was a pretty big guy and he could run.

Well, whenever we played up in Fenway Park in Boston, Jimmy had a habit of hitting line drives off that green wall in left field and most of the time he would just make the turn at first and hold up with a single. I got after him one day and said, 'Jimmy, you know, you could help the ballclub sometimes if you would use some of your speed to turn those hits off the wall into doubles.' He just sort of smiled. Then, on the last day of the season, we had this special day of events with the Yankees. You know, hitting contests, throwing contests, and the sort. One of the events was a 100 yard dash and the prize was $100. I was the favorite to win, although a few of the Yankees and our own Sam Chapman would give me a good run. Well, I got a great start and was leading the field when, at about the 80 yard mark I hear some heavy footsteps closing ground. I thought sure it must be Chapman, who was a great runner, but, before I knew it, Jimmy Foxx had passed me and won the race easily!"

Later, during an autograph session in which Bill was inundated with autograph seekers, I had a chance to meet and speak with one of his sons, who had accompanied Bill to the meeting. I mentioned my telephone conversation with his father almost 2 years earlier and expressed how pleased I was to see his father in such apparently high spirits after the experience of losing his wife and his leg at about the same time.

"Yes, Dad's doing really well. He and mom were married for 70 years and now he has a new girlfriend! He's like a Timex watch. 'Takes a lickin' and keeps on tickin'."

RAY CRONE
Waxahachie, TX
May, 2002

Ray `walks out onto the front lawn of his small ranch style home when he sees me drive up. He invites me to bring my things inside.

"I live here by myself now," he says. "My wife died a couple of years ago."

I inquire about the circumstances of his wife's passing.

"Well, a lot of things just caught up with her. She actually died of kidney failure, after being on dialysis for a couple of years, but she was also a diabetic and had had a 3-way heart bypass operation. I think delivering 4 children was just more than her body was able to handle," Ray explains, as we sit in a sunroom at the back of his house.

"Tell me a little about your career and how you wound up with the Giants," I say.

"I had the misfortune of coming up with the Milwaukee Braves in the mid-'50s," Ray begins. "They had Warren Spahn, Lew Burdette, Bob Buhl, Gene Conley, Ernie Johnson, and Chet Nichols. You weren't going to get a lot of work on a staff like that. They did like to pitch me in Ebbets Field though. They didn't like to pitch Spahn there because of the short left field wall and the right-hand hitting Dodger lineup, although Spahn was usually more effective against right hand hitters than against lefties. Anyway, in mid-1957, when we were in Philadelphia, I got word that I had been traded to the Giants. I came back from dinner one night at the hotel and there was a message in my box from John Quinn, the general manager, that I had been traded to the Giants, along with Danny O'Connell, and Bobby Thomson. My wife, back in Milwaukee, heard about it on the radio before I even got the message. I always loved playing in the Polo Grounds, but I didn't do much with the Giants. I finished out the '57 season with them, but (Bill) Rigney didn't seem to have a place for me in his plans for '58 and I eventually was shipped back to the minors and never got back to the big leagues." Ray adds, "I guess a lot of it was my own fault," although he does not elaborate.

"What do you think of the game today?" I ask.

"Oh, it's not the same at all. Everything's changed. The umpires make up their own strike zone and money is all that matters. I think that the coming of television ruined the game. It made players and umpires into actors and is at the heart of all the financial issues and greed that are part of baseball now," Ray observes.

Before I leave, Ray takes me into the living room and shows me his collection of photos from his playing days. One shows a very young Ray Crone standing next to an aged Babe Ruth and two others, with an airplane in the background. "That picture was taken in 1948, not long before Babe died. I was a high school pitcher in Memphis at the time and was invited to have my picture taken with him," Ray explains.

Another of his favorites is a photo of his attractive young wife, taken in the Polo Grounds. She is smiling and holding a cigarette in her hand. In the background can be seen the big Chesterfield cigarette sign that dominated the centerfield section of the Polo Grounds.

JOHNNY EDWARDS
Houston, TX
May, 2002

It is mid-evening on Mother's Day when a relaxed and smiling John Edwards, young granddaughter at his side, comes to the door in answer to my visit. I introduce myself, apologize for stopping by unannounced, and explain the purpose of my visit. Still smiling and extending his hand in greeting, John welcomes me and immediately introduces me to his granddaughter, explaining that she too is a ballplayer and has just completed a very successful season with her girls' team. In enthusiastic response to my inquiry, she fills me in on the highlights of the recently completed tournament game in which she has played. Then, returning to the purpose of my visit, John says, "Oh yes, I'm used to all this. Hardly a day goes by that I don't get something in the mail to sign. I must be the only ballplayer not doing shows and charging for autographs."

Knowing that he grew up in Columbus, Ohio, not far from where I grew up, I mention the fact that we were playing high school baseball at about the same time and ask him about a story that I had heard.

"John, I remember a story that either Waite Hoyt (Cincinnati Reds broadcaster) or Vin Scully (LA Dodgers broadcaster) told about your experience with Jack Nicklaus as a high school baseball player. Can you fill me in on that?" I ask.

Grinning, John begins, "Oh, sure. Jack grew up in Columbus and he was a hell of a baseball catcher. In 1955, when Jack was a sophomore in high school and I was a junior, playing at a high school across town, Jack was selected as the first team All-State catcher in Ohio and I was the second team All-State catcher. It was in the summer of '55 that Jack decided to devote all of his time to golf, so he dropped out of baseball after that season. So, in 1956, which was my senior year, I was selected as the first team All-State catcher in Ohio, but it was only because Jack had given up the sport! I would never have received that honor if Jack Nicklaus hadn't switched from baseball to golf, but things worked out pretty well for both of us."

Then, picking up on the fact that I was a contemporary who had grown up in Dayton, John inquires, "Did you ever know a fellow named Ron Nischwitz?"

"Sure. He was a tall left-handed pitcher at Fairview High School. I played against him in high school. He pitched for Detroit for a few years," I reply.

"Yes. Ron's a good friend of mine. We used to work out together a lot. Small world," John observes.

John has some problems with the pen I have given him to sign the ball and asks his daughter, who has now joined us, with her husband, to bring him a ballpoint pen from inside the house. While we are waiting for her to return, I ask John for his thoughts about the game today.

"Well, all the money has changed the game. It's just not the same. Do you know that in 1961, when the Reds team I was playing on won the National League championship and played in the World Series, the payroll for the entire ballclub was $2 million! And today there are individual players making 10 times that much in a single season...and they don't play the game as well! Ballplayers used to spend a lot of time together. Now, all of their time is taken up by their agents and investment advisors," John says.

It's getting dark and the mosquitoes are starting to bite, so John finishes signing my items and we conclude our visit.

Two months after my visit with John, I received a note in the mail from him postmarked July 5, 2002. The note read: "Thanks for your note. To this day, my kids can't believe that you came all the way from Irving for an 'old' catcher's autograph." Also enclosed were three autographed photos of John in different team uniforms (Cardinals, Reds, Astros).

CARL ERSKINE **"Oisk"**
Cincinnati, OH
April 2003

A lot has been said and written about Carl Erskine and of his being one of the consummate gentlemen of the game of baseball. He was always one of my favorite Dodger players (and I hated the Dodgers when I was growing up), and I consider it a true privilege to have had the opportunity to meet Carl on several occasions and get to know him rather well. Beyond my respect for his baseball playing abilities, I have particular admiration for the manner in which Carl and his wife, Betty, have raised their youngest child, a son named Jimmy, who was born on April 1, 1960, with Down syndrome. At the time of Jimmy's birth, the life expectancy of a Down syndrome inflicted child was, at best, 20-30 years, and most such afflicted children were institutionalized. The Erskines, however, chose to raise Jimmy themselves, making all of the necessary personal sacrifices to ensure the best care possible for him. On April 1, 2003, Jimmy celebrated his 43rd birthday. He lives at home with his parents and they drive him daily to his job at Applebee's and to his swimming exercises. They are truly very special people and I always make it a point to inquire about Jimmy when I have an opportunity to visit with Carl.

I have some new subjects to discuss with Carl during this visit, where he is signing autographs at a card show at

Moeller High School. As always, I ask him how Jimmy is doing.

"Ah, Jimmy's doing great. He was 43 on April 1 and he has now finished his fouth year of working at Applebee's. They had a little celebration for him the other day and he really enjoyed that. Thanks for asking about him."

I ask Carl if he has read the new biography of Sandy Koufax, Sandy Koufax, A Lefty's Legacy, and mention that I did not realize that Koufax had been such a student of pitching mechanics, as was suggested in the book.

"Well, I don't really think he was. The author (Jane Leavy) contacted me for some information and I was sort of reluctant to say much out of respect for Sandy's known sense of privacy, but I recall his saying to me at the beginning of the 1960 season that he was thinking about giving the game up. He said he thought he would give it one more year and, if things weren't a lot better, then he was probably going to call it quits. He certainly managed to turn things around. Once he gained confidence in his control, he was one of those rare pitchers who could survive on one pitch. If he couldn't get his curve ball over, he'd just throw that fast ball and challenge the hitter to hit it. Not many could!"

Carl continues on the subject of books about pitching. "You know, Roger Kahn, who wrote The Boys Of Summer, also recently wrote a book about pitching called The Head Game. Koufax and Drysdale were both subjects in that book. Roger asked me to review the book and share my thoughts about it with him. I told him I thought he had written about the wrong pitchers. Guys like Koufax and Drysdale didn't have to use their heads to succeed. They had an abundance of natural talent. The real "heady" pitchers were guys like Warren Spahn, Whitey Ford, Preacher Roe, Lew Burdette, and even Robin Roberts for most of his career. Those were the guys who learned how to beat you by using their heads instead of their arms."

At one time I had asked Tommy Henrich whether he thought Joe Dimaggio or Mickey Mantle was the better hitter, so I posed the same question to Erskine.

"I really didn't have much experience with DiMaggio. Faced him once in a World Series game and got him out on a high fly ball. I saw a lot of Mantle though and I had pretty good luck with him. Struck him out 4 times in one game in the '53 Series. As a matter of fact, one of the few hits he got off me was when he bunted for a base hit with two outs and two strikes on him. A few years later I was playing in a golf outing with some of the Yankee players and mentioned to them that Mickey must not have known the situation when he did that. They just laughed and said that he knew perfectly well what the situation was and that he had said before he went to bat, 'If that little son-of-a-bitch gets two strikes on me, I know he's going to throw me that god-damned curve ball and, when he does, I'm going to bunt my way on.'"

Carl continues with his thoughts. "You know, it's funny how some pitchers have certain batter's numbers and some batters have certain pitcher's numbers. Orlando Cepeda used to wear out Lew Burdette. Hit everything he threw up there. Burdette just couldn't get Cepeda out. So one day Burdette told his catcher, Del Crandall, to tell Cepeda what pitch was coming before every pitch. All of a sudden he starts having better success pitching to Cepeda. Sometimes you have to do strange things."

GENE STEPHENS
Ft. Worth, TX
June, 2003

I'm looking at golf clubs when Gene Stephens arrives at the Tourline Golf Shop in southwest Ft. Worth. I recognize the Mercedes coupe he told me he would be driving when we arranged the meeting. Gene lives 30-40 miles further south in Granbury, but offered to meet me in Ft. Worth to shorten my trip. He often shops at Tourline and wanted to order a new golf club anyway. He is wearing golf shorts, a casual Hawaiian print shirt, and his hair is cut in a '50s brush cut. I introduce myself when he enters the store and we fall naturally into conversation, which is a continuation of our telephone visit earlier in the day.

"So, where was it you saw Grady Hatton?" Gene asks.

"I visited with Grady at his farm over in Warren, Texas a year or two ago. He was wearing his bib overalls and seemed to be in pretty good shape. We had a nice visit together," I reply.

"Well, as you probably know, Grady finished out his playing days in Boston while I was still with the Red Sox. He was a real gentleman. Very clean. Didn't drink or run around. Just a real nice fellow. Unfortunately, not all of the younger players appreciated Grady's being there. We had a young "bonus baby" named Billy Consolo who thought he was ready to be the starting third baseman and he, in particular, didn't much like Grady because Grady kept him from playing much," Gene offers. "In those days there were a lot more good ballplayers competing for a limited number of big league positions, so the youngsters often resented the older players who could still play and kept them from breaking in."

Gene continues, "I went through something similar myself. I played the outfield for Boston while Ted Williams was in Korea and when he returned in 1953, I became the fourth outfielder for the Red Sox. I was a pretty decent player, but they had Ted Williams, Jimmy Piersall, and Jackie Jensen. That was a pretty strong group, so I wound up playing 120 games a year, getting 60-70 at bats, as a defensive substitution. It was tough and I never really felt that I was able to develop my full potential as a ballplayer in that situation, but Williams was a great hitter, Piersall an excellent outfielder, and Jensen was the all-around athlete. No room for Stephens to start in that group."

I query, "As great a hitter as Williams was, it seemed to me that he never really played well against the Yankees. I never remember his tormenting the Yankees with his bat like (Joe) DiMaggio did to the Red Sox time after time. Is my impression accurate?"

"Yes, but there is a simple explanation for that. Allie Reynolds said it best when he said that the Yankee strategy was never to let Williams beat them. So the reality of the situation was that the Yankee pitchers seldom gave Williams, who was a notoriously selective hitter anyway, anything good to hit," Gene explains.

"What about Piersall?' I ask.

"He was a very fine outfielder. Fast. Covered a lot of ground. Knew how to play the outfield. Of course, he made a lot of plays look more difficult than they were. Dom DiMaggio, Piersall's predecessor in center field, made everything look easier than it really was. Piersall was the opposite; he made everything look harder than it was. And he was very protective of his position. I used to have to fight him for time in the batting cage. He didn't want to let me hit. He considered me a threat to his position, which, of course, I was. I finally took over his job, but it was only because he got injured."

"What do you think of the game today?" I ask.

"I don't think much of it. The players today don't really know the game the way it used to be. They don't do the basic things we used to have to do to win, like sacrifice, hit behind runners to allow them to advance, throw to the proper base, and stuff like that. They all just want to hit the ball out of the park. I watch the (Texas) Rangers play and realize that they just don't really know how to win. I don't have much interest in the game anymore. It was a part of my life that's behind me. I guess I'm a little disappointed that I never really got to develop what I thought was my full potential as a big league ballplayer," Gene laments.

Gene agrees to our having a photograph taken by one of the clerks in the shop and then I wish him luck with the new driver he is planning to purchase as we part company.

MARTY MARION
St. Louis, MO
October, 2003

Marty is a tall, slender, and talkative southern gentleman. His friendly, outgoing nature fits perfectly with his large southern style home in Ladue, an upscale St. Louis suburb. His pleasant manner and smooth mobility belie his 86 years. He welcomes me into his home with a smile and a handshake and insists that we sit down in the living room, where we can talk and not be distracted by the Texas Tech-Missouri football game that he has been watching in the family room. He is giving me his full and undivided attention.

As he looks carefully at the autographs on the St. Louis Cardinals bat that I have brought for him to sign, he chuckles over Enos Slaughter's signature. "You know," he says, "old 'Country' (Slaughter's nickname) was one of a kind. I don't know what he would have done if he hadn't played baseball. He got more out of limited natural ability than about anyone I've ever known, but he was one tough competitor. He was a terrible fielder. I remember a game we were playing one day when Red Barrett was pitching and 'Country' misplayed a ground ball in the outfield from a single into a triple. When the inning was over and he came into the dugout Barrett went over and offered 'Country' his glove. 'Do you think this would help you?' Barrett said. 'Aw, shit! The ball hit a Coke bottle, Red,' Country responded."

I mention the famous photograph of Slaughter sliding across home plate with the winning run in the final game of the 1946 World Series, the culmination of his mad dash from first to home on Harry Walker's single. The photo shows Marion, the next batter, watching Slaughter's slide, as Roy Partee, the Red Sox catcher, waits for the throw and the umpire prepares to signal Slaughter "safe."

Marty smiles and chuckles again. "Yes, when Enos got up and passed me on his way back to the dugout I said, 'What was your hurry Country? I was going to hit you in anyway.' Country said, 'I wasn't takin' no chances!'"

Marty continues, "You know, I ran into Stan (Musial) a few months ago and he had gone over to somewhere in the Carolinas to attend Enos' funeral earlier this year. Stan said to me, 'Marty, you're not going to believe this, but Enos was buried in his baseball uniform.'"

Marty asks me about my collection, how I got started with it, and how I've managed to obtain so many autographs. He tells me that he gets calls all the time from dealers who want to buy memorabilia items from him, but that he only has two items from his playing days. He says he wants to show them to me. He walks me across the living room to a bookcase and points out a pair of bookends at either end of a row of books. The bookends are in the shape of human hands, a right hand on one end and a left hand on the other. He takes one of the bookends from the shelf and hands it to me. It is a true work of art. "Feel this," he says. It is a solid bronze casting and is extremely heavy. The hand is done in great detail, including wrinkles and veins. While I am holding it, Marty points out a ring that is cast into the ring finger. "That's a 1944 World Series ring," he says and then proceeds with his story.

"'Doc' Weaver was the club trainer when I was with the Cardinals and he took good care of all of the players. He was one of the best known trainers in the league at that time. He used to spend a lot of time working on my back before and after games. When I retired as a player from the Cardinals, 'Doc' had a mold made of his hands and then had these bookends made for me," Marty explained.

The bookends are magnificent and probably the most unique gift I have seen. Marty is understandably proud of them and, after replacing the one he had handed me, he leads me out of the living room into his family room and shows me the plaque commemorating his selection as the National League's Most Valuable Player in 1944. It is a large bronze piece mounted on a black rectangular ground. It is named the Kenesaw Mountain Landis Award. Marty explains: "In 1944 the war was still on and materials were hard to come by. So, at the award ceremony, I was given a piece of cardboard that included a drawing of what the award looked like. I didn't receive the actual plaque until two years later, when the war was over and the materials for it could be obtained. I've been offered $50,000 for that plaque by several memorabilia dealers, but my family would shoot me if I even considered letting it go."

Before leaving the family room, Marty invites my attention to a large aerial photograph of a farm with a large lake, surrounded by many trees, that is on the wall. He explains that the property is in Illinois, about an hour and a half's drive, and is his "home away from home." It is an 80-acre parcel. He points out that the lake has 13 separate fingers and coves and says that his wife loves to fish those coves.

I've had a wonderful visit with a real gentleman and one of the game's great ballplayers. I thank Marty for his time and hospitality as he shakes my hand when we part.

MEL PARNELL
New Orleans, LA
January, 2004

It's a sunny mid-afternoon when I arrive at the well maintained single story home on a corner lot across the street from a beautiful community park in Lakeview, an upper middle class neighborhood on the north side of the city. It is a remarkably serene setting. Mel answers the door with a smile and a handshake, invites me inside and to have a seat in the living room. We've met previously at a signing show in St. Louis several years ago and recall briefly the event. Mel takes a seat in a nearby chair, crosses his legs, and, in a relaxed manner, lets me start conversation.

"Well, what do you think of the game today?" I ask.

"It's quite different," he begins. "The talent is diluted and there are too many minor leaguers playing in the majors. Specialization is another thing. Take pitching, for instance. Hardly anyone pitches a complete game anymore. You have starters, middle relievers, set-up relievers, and closers. And it seems to me that the closers get most of the attention. When we were playing, pitchers were expected to pitch the entire game. Nowadays a starting pitcher is only expected to go 4-5 innings."

"Yes, I read recently that Robin Roberts pitched 29 consecutive complete games one year," I add. "You don't see that these days."

"Right! I remember starting 39 games and finishing 27 of them one year (1949)," Mel responds, then adds, "I also think the game has been taken away from the fans. It's all about money and, at least in Boston, only the big corporations can afford the ticket prices. The owners in Boston are committed to staying in Fenway Park. The latest plan is to add seats on top of the grandstand roof in right field. Those seats will cost $50 per game. Not too many ordinary fans can afford that, so they kind of get shut out," Mel observes.

"Speaking of Fenway, how did you like pitching in that park?" I ask. (The short distance to the wall in left field, infamously known as the 'green monster,' has generally been thought to be a major obstacle for left-handed pitchers pitching to right-handed batters. Parnell is a 'lefty'.)

"I loved pitching in Fenway and generally had great success there," he says, warming to the subject. "I just pitched everyone inside. Some thought I was crazy, but I broke a lot of bats. Think about it. Most right-handed hitters can't generate a lot of power when they can't extend their arms and if you make a mistake inside its not going to kill you. Of course, I'd throw outside now and then to keep hitters honest, but never with a strike. I haven't had much luck convincing Boston's recent left-handers to pitch inside. I tried to get Bob Ojeda and John Tudor to work inside, but they wouldn't try it. The only guy who listened to me was Bruce Hurst and he said, 'By golly, you CAN win pitching inside in this park.'"

"How did you do against DiMaggio and Mantle?" I follow.

"I did very well. They didn't hurt me that bad. DiMaggio only hit 4 homers off me. Mantle was terribly strong. One night in Fenway he hit a ball out in deep right center field, the deepest part of the park, against one of our guys. When he hit the ball, the park became deathly quiet and everyone could hear our catcher say, 'My god, look at that thing go!' After Mantle hit that 565 foot homer out of Griffith Stadium in Washington one of our guys asked the Senators' catcher if he thought the wind helped carry it so far. He said, 'Hell, the wind couldn't catch up with it!'"

At this point I give Mel my copy of The Summer of '49 to autograph and the conversation turns to the last two games of that season, when the Yankees won the last two games against the Red Sox to win the pennant. Mel signs over a picture of himself and, as he looks over the other pictures on the facing page he notices Ellis Kinder, prompting him to say, "Man, there was one tough cookie. He was a real pitcher and competitor, but Ellis and I were exhausted at the end of that year. The two of us pitched a hell of a lot of games down the stretch and we just didn't have much left at the end. But Ellis was a trooper and he could pitch better hung over than most guys could sober. One night when he was scheduled to pitch, Ellis came to the park drunk as a skunk. We had to hide him from McCarthy and after he warmed up he didn't bother to go back into the clubhouse to change his uniform shirt, because he couldn't have made it there and back. When he took the mound to start the game, he started his windup and, when his hands got over his head, he fell backward off the mound," Mel recalls, chuckling.

Mel's thoughts return to the Yankees. "You know, the Yankees in those days had an awful lot of talent and those guys were BIG! In addition to DiMaggio they had Johnny Mize, Charlie Keller, Billy Johnson, Johnny Lindell, Cliff

Mapes, Hank Bauer, Gene Woodling, and Tommy Henrich. Whenever you got one of them out, you were looking at another. They just kept coming. I'll never forget Tommy Henrich. The first time I pitched against the Yankees in Yankee Stadium I threw a perfect pitch, knee high on the outside corner and Henrich hit it into the seats in right field for a home run. While Henrich was circling the bases, the home plate umpire, Cal Hubbard, came halfway to the mound to deliver a new ball to me. 'If you keep pitching that way you'll win a lot of ball games, young man,' he said. Maybe so, but it didn't turn out so well that time, I replied."

Mel continues, "The Yankees and us had very equal teams in those days, but they had one man who was the difference. That was Joe Page. Joe Page was the guy who made the difference between our clubs in 1949. We just didn't have someone who could come in and take over a game like Page did for the Yankees that year. We tried to make a deal to get Max Surkont that year. Most of the players thought he could help our staff a lot, sort of like Page did for the Yankees. But our management wouldn't make the deal. We sure could have used him."

We finish our meeting with some conversation about a couple of Mel's teammates, Ted Williams and Bobby Doerr. Mel invites me to join him for lunch the following day. He is meeting with several former ballplayer friends, George Strickland, Gene Freese, Ralph Caballero and a couple of others at a place called Zeke's. I thank him for the invitation and for letting me stop by, but I have an appointment with Matt Batts in Baton Rouge and have to decline.

"PUTSY" CABALLERO
New Orleans, LA
January, 2004

"Putsy" is standing in the yard looking for me when I drive up. We had agreed to a 4:00 PM meeting and my conversation with Mel Parnell has made me a few minutes late.

"Hope you didn't get lost," he says as I get out of the car.

"No, your directions were great. I just got tied up a little longer than I anticipated," I reply.

"Come on in, I've got some things to show you," he says leading me into the kitchen and introducing me to his wife, daughter, and granddaughter on the way. He takes me to the kitchen table where he has spread out some newspaper clippings and photographs. The first thing he shows me is a photo, taken from the internet, showing a baseball that he has autographed and added a notation that reads: 'Youngest third baseman to play in the major leagues…April, 1944…16 years old.' He says, "Some fellow sent me a ball and asked me to autograph it and include that information. I remember signing it. Now he's trying to sell it on the internet. A relative of mine saw it and sent it to me." He seems more amused than upset by the matter. I tell him that several of the players I have visited have expressed concern over this sort of thing and a few have refused to sign anything if they think it is going to be sold.

Next he shows me an action photo that was taken in 1948 during a game between the Phillies and the Brooklyn Dodgers. It shows "Putsy" reaching to put the tag on a sliding Jackie Robinson at third base. He describes the play: "Jackie was on third and he was taking his usual daring lead, trying to upset the pitcher, running back and forth down the baseline. The batter hit a grounder to third and I knew that Jackie would make a break for home as soon as I released the throw to first. So, I cocked my arm and faked the throw to first and hustled over to the bag to tag Jackie trying to get back to third. As you can see, it looks like he beat the tag, but the umpire called him out. That photo wasn't printed for 50 years until USA Today ran it a few years ago in memory of Jackie's joining the Dodgers in 1947."

I pick up on the opportunity. "So you were playing when Ben Chapman managed the Phillies. I understand he got pretty ugly about Robinson."

Putsy jumps right in. "Oh boy, did he ever! We had a standing rule on our club in 1948. Jackie had moved to second base that year, his normal position. Chapman told our guys that anyone who went into second base and didn't try to take Jackie out would be fined $500, which was a lot of money in those days. It was nasty stuff. We had one fellow who flew out to the outfield. He rounded first base and, as he circled past Jackie on his way back to the dugout said to Robinson, 'Hang in there, Jackie. Not all of us believe in this shit.' It was so bad that we wound up hurting our own team. Andy Seminick injured a leg trying to take Robinson out and one of our outfielders dislocated a shoulder trying to do the same thing. We did more damage to ourselves than we were ever able to do to Jackie."

Somehow, Marty Marion's name is mentioned and Putsy exclaims, "Now there's a guy who should be in the Hall of Fame. Everyone talks about that guy Ozzie Smith, but, hell, he got to play on a carpet over there. Never had to deal with a bad hop. Marion played on that rock quarry in Sportsman's Park and you never knew what the ball was going to do on that infield. I remember sitting in the dugout over there, which sat a little below the level of the playing field, and being able to see light between the bottom of (Cardinal's third baseman) Whitey Kurowski's shoes and the surface of the infield. That infield was so hard his spikes didn't penetrate it!"

Putsy shows me two recent Polaroid pictures, one of his wife and one of himself, each with Pete Rose. I ask him what he thinks of the Pete Rose situation.

"Well, I don't think they should let him back into baseball. What do you think?" Putsy asks.

"I think they should probably maintain the suspension, but I don't know how baseball can just ignore what the guy accomplished as a player. I grew up around Pete and Pete was not blessed with a great amount of natural talent. He had to work hard to become the player that he was. It's really a shame that he didn't handle things better than he did, because he could have been a wonderful example for a lot of young kids. He just made some terrible decisions. I think they should put him into the Hall of Fame and include on his plaque that he was banned from baseball for life after his playing days were over," I submit.

"Yeah, maybe so," Putsy says.

Then he goes to a drawer and takes out a picture of himself in his 1950 Phillies uniform, autographs it with a personalization, and hands it to me. "Here, take this with you," he says. "I wish we could visit some more, but I've got to take this group (his family) out to dinner and the Hornets game tonight."

He walks to the car with me and I thank him for the visit and the picture.

GEORGE STRICKLAND
New Orleans, LA
January, 2004

George's phone number is unlisted, so I had been unable to arrange a meeting with him until "Putsy" Caballero gave me the number during my visit with him. "Putsy" encouraged me to call George, saying he was a wonderful fellow and would be glad to hear from me. Reinforced by "Putsy's" encouragement, I called George late the afternoon before I was to leave New Orleans. The experience that followed is one that I will not forget.

After introducing myself and explaining the purpose of my phone call, George says to me "Well, my wife has Alzheimer's so I'm here at home pretty much 24/7. We'll be eating dinner shortly and I usually put her to bed about 9:00 o'clock. If you'd like to come by around 8:00 PM, that would be okay with me. Only thing is, don't be surprised if I have my pajamas on."

"Oh, that's alright. Maybe I'll bring mine and we can have a pajama party," I kid. "I'll see you around 8:00."

The house is a classic older multi-story southern home near the end of a heavily tree lined street that ends at the edge of Audubon Park. I climb the stairs to the front porch, ring the bell, and in a few seconds George answers and, sure enough, he is wearing his pajamas, robe, and house slippers. He welcomes me with a handshake and a warm smile and leads me into the living room. I am a little surprised to see George's wife, Loraine, comfortably resting in a reclined easy chair. She is covered with a blanket and awake, but she appears almost unresponsive to our presence. Although George had mentioned the situation to me, I did not anticipate the extent of her incapacity. George introduces me and I thank them both for letting me stop in, but she gives no response. Smiling, George says to her in a tender way, "We're just going to talk about baseball for a little while, dear."

George motions me to a seat on the sofa and sits down next to me. Looking at the signatures on one of the bats I have brought for him to sign he says, "Virgil Trucks! I'll never forgive you, Virgil." He looks at me and explains, "In 1952 I was with the Indians and Virgil was with the Tigers. That's the year he was 5-19 and pitched 2 no-hitters. We were playing in Detroit and it was right after he had pitched one of his no-hitters. He got our leadoff man out, but then gave up six consecutive singles. I'm hitting eighth and, as I walk to the plate, I know what's coming. Matt Batts was the catcher and I said to him, 'Matt, tell Virgil I had a bad night last night and not to knock me down because I don't think I can get away from it.' Well, sure enough, Virgil throws that fastball right here. (He puts his hand next to my left shoulder.) So, when you see Batts tomorrow, tell him 'hello' for me and that I still haven't forgiven him and Virgil for that."

When he looks at the bat autographed by Pittsburgh Pirates, George is reminded of Murry Dickson. "Not too long ago I received a request in the mail for an autograph. The letter was obviously written by a youngster and, judging by the name 'Allie,' I assume it was a girl. Anyway, she went on to say that I was one of her favorite ballplayers, because I had played with her great-grandfather, Murry Dickson. It kinda' hit me that I had never thought of myself as being old enough to have played with someone's great-grandfather!"

He continues, "You know, when I was at Pittsburgh, Honus Wagner used to come out to the games once in awhile. He'd come into the clubhouse, sit down on a stool, and the clubhouse boys would help him put on his uniform. Then he'd go out and usually sit with the fellows down in the bullpen. I always called him Mr. Wagner and he'd say, 'Call me Hans or Honus.' Anyway, I asked him how the current players compared with the players of his day. He said, 'Oh, the players today are better.'"

"Well George, let me ask you that same question," I say.

He thinks about the question for a moment and then responds, "I think the players today are much bigger, stronger, and faster than in my day, but I don't think they play the game the same way or have the same commitment to the game that we had. It's not so much a team game anymore. The money has changed everything. Everyone's looking out for himself. They all want private hotel rooms, even suites, and stuff like that. We traveled by train and had roommates in the hotels. Our whole life was baseball. I think about that young kid (Darryl Kile) who died alone in his hotel room a year or so ago, and wonder whether he might still be alive if he had had a roommate. So, I guess I'd say they are better athletes, but not necessarily better baseball players."

A sort of short moan comes from Mrs. Strickland. George smiles and speaks to her lovingly, "Yes, that's right. It's okay, sweetie."

I take the conversation to the 1954 World Series. "George, what happened with the Indians in the '54 Series?"

He smiles as he looks at me. "Well, I guess that depends on who you talk to. I think the Giants had a great team and we ran into some great pitching from them in that Series. Rosen has always said that the pressure we put on ourselves to win 111 games and set the regular season record made the World Series sort of anti-climactic. It's hard to think that you'd downplay a World Series, but its true that we went all out to win those 111 games."

"Did the catch by Mays in the first game have a big impact?" I ask.

George replies, "That catch was the most overblown thing I've ever seen. It was strictly showboat. I've seen a lot of catches better than that. If you watch that play closely, you'll see he actually slowed down before he caught the ball. He DID run like hell to get there, but he could have turned around to make the catch. The play wasn't that tough."

George goes to another room and returns to show me a black-and-white lithograph. The artist has sketched the portraits of the Cleveland pitching staff in 1954 (Bob Feller, Bob Lemon, Early Wynn, Mike Garcia) and manager Al Lopez. Each has autographed the print.

"Tell me about that pitching staff," I say.

George explains, "I roomed with 'Big Mike' (Garcia) for several years. He was just a big, strong, powerful pitcher and he threw a very 'heavy' ball. Lemon was more of a finesse pitcher. He had great control and had the speed when he needed it. He was a great pitcher to play behind. Wynn was another matter. He had very good control, but he liked to 'nibble' and he was forever going deep into the count, 3 and 1, 3 and 2. When you played behind Wynn, you were just exhausted by the end of the game. Feller was pretty much just closing out his career. His better days were behind him."

A glance at my watch tells me its 9:00, so I start gathering my stuff to leave.

"Did you say you saw Parnell today?" George asks.

"Yes, I visited with him this afternoon," I reply.

"You know," George says, "he and I were married on the same day. I got married in the morning and he got married in the afternoon. We went to high school together. I always kid him about not coming to my wedding. He says, 'Well, you didn't come to mine either.'"

As he prepares to walk me to the door, he stops and leans over to talk softly and sweetly to his wife. He tells me they have been married for 56 years. She started with Alzheimer's eleven years ago and 3 years ago she suffered a broken hip from osteoporosis. She has glaucoma in one eye and has lost all of her teeth. Her eyes remain clear, but are unresponsive. The love he shows to her is so transparent and beautiful. Much as I have enjoyed talking baseball with George, it is the relationship between him and his wife that has made a deep and unforgettable impression upon me.

MATT BATTS
Baton Rouge, LA
January, 2004

The Country Club of Louisiana is an upscale, gated community just south of Baton Rouge. Once cleared by the guard at the main gate, I enjoy the scenic drive through the tree lined streets, past lakes and fountains, to Matt and Arleene Batts' home on a corner in a quiet neighborhood. When Matt opens the front door, an energetic golden retriever bolts out of the house, past me, and across the street through a neighbor's side yard. Matt invites me in, introduces me to his wife, Arleene, and directs me to the sofa in the living room. Arleene excuses herself to go find the dog while Matt inquires about my visit with his friends in New Orleans. I tell him that George Strickland hasn't forgiven him and Virgil Trucks for the knockdown in '52. Matt chuckles.

A few minutes later, Arleene appears at the patio door, which is locked, with the dog in tow. I get up to unlock and open the door for them. Once back inside, Arleene points to a book that is displayed on a bookstand on the coffee table in front of the sofa and says, "Are you familiar with The Summer of '49?"

It was the first thing I had noticed upon entering the living room when I arrived. I knew immediately from the dust cover that it was a first edition copy of David Halberstam's classic documentary of the 1949 American League pennant race. It is one of my favorite books and Halberstam is my favorite author. I have brought a special, leather bound edition of the book with me for Matt to autograph.

"Oh, yes," I reply, showing her my own special edition of the book. "David Halberstam is my all-time favorite writer. I think I've read almost every book he's written."

"Have you read the one about the firefighters?" she asks, holding up a copy of Firehouse, a tribute to the firemen from a local engine house, all but one of whom died in the WTC disaster on 9-11-01. "David lives right around the corner from the firehouse and knew those fellows."

It turns out that Matt and Arleene have become friends with Halberstam from the research that he did with Matt on The Summer of '49. Matt picks up the story. "When he was here interviewing me, I asked him if he would like a Coke or something to drink. He said he'd like that and when I brought him a coke in one of those old green Coca-Cola bottles he got real excited. 'Oh, my! You've really made my day,' he said."

Arleene then adds, "A few years ago our daughter went to New York and David got her front row seats to one of the

Broadway shows and she took him a carton of Cokes in the old bottles."

The conversation swings back to the last game of the '49 season as I say to Matt, "According to the book, you weren't too happy about McCarthy's pulling Kinder for a pinch-hitter in that game. What were your thoughts?"

"Well, first of all, I was one of McCarthy's little 'bobo's.' He and I got along fine and I liked him as a manager. But Kinder had only given up that one run in the first inning and was really pitching well. The Yankees hadn't done much with him and I didn't think it made much sense to take him out under such circumstances," Matt answers.

"Who was the best pitcher you ever caught?" I pose.

"Satchel Paige, without a doubt," Matt replies immediately. "Satch could throw every pitch you've ever heard of and put the ball right where he wanted it. I'll never forget one day when I was catching him with the (St. Louis) Browns. We were playing Cleveland and, for some reason, Satchel and Larry Doby really hated each other. Doby comes to bat late in the game with a couple of men on base and a chance to win the game with a hit. Ol' Satch gets 2 strikes on Doby and then motions me out to the mound and says to me, 'Batts, you put down however many fingers you want to, but I'm not throwing the pitch you signal for. I don't like this nigger and I'm going to throw him my 'hesitation' pitch.' So Satch gets set and at the very top of his delivery he literally stopped his motion for a split second and then blew a fast ball right past Doby, who had started his stride way ahead of the pitch. Damnest thing I ever saw!"

"Another thing," Matt continues, "Satch knew how to use the pitching rubber. He used the whole thing. He didn't pitch from one spot, like most pitchers do. He moved around. For left-handed hitters he liked to use the extreme right-hand side of the rubber and for right-handed hitters he used the other side. He said that most hitters didn't like to see the ball boring in on them. The guy just knew about everything there was to know about pitching."

Matt warms to the subject of Paige and continues, "After a game Satch would always wait until everyone else had showered before getting in the shower with me and one of the other players. He'd turn the shower on full hot, no cold mixed in, and even his black skin got red. The water was so hot that it would burn you if you were showering nearby and it splashed on you. He told me he had done that since he was a kid and that it was the way he took care of his arm. 'I don't use none of that rub on my arm like those other guys do. Just hot water,' he said."

I mention that I got to see Satchel pitch in the 1953 All-Star Game in Cincinnati when I was a kid and wonder how old Satch was at that time. Arleene says, "Well, let's see." She goes to the bookshelf, takes down a baseball encyclopedia, and quickly determines that Paige was born in 1906.

"Wow, if that's right, he was 47 years old," I marvel.

Arleene encourages Matt to show me his memorabilia. He first takes me to the other side of the living room where a large glass enclosed case contains his old catcher's equipment (mask, chest protector, shin guards, spikes, and catcher's mitt), several autographed balls, and a fielder's glove. He opens the door to the case and hands me the fielder's glove. The glove reveals a fair amount of use, the webbing between the thumb and fingers has been torn loose, and part of the heel of the glove is ripped. Matt explains, "I had a couple of terriers that got hold of this one time when I left it out. They sort of worked it over."

Examining the glove, I notice that it is a Bob Dillinger model glove. The back of the glove contains 12-15 autographs of former Red Sox players: Ted Williams, Bobby Doerr, Johnny Pesky, Billy Goodman, Walt Dropo, Maurice McDermott, Dom DiMaggio, and others. Matt tells me that the glove was given to him by Ted Williams. Then he hands me his old catcher's mitt and tells me that, at one point it had been lost or stolen. He received a phone call one day from a fellow who said he had obtained the mitt by way of purchase or an auction and would be glad to return it to Matt, if he wanted it. Matt said he was somewhat skeptical, but, when the mitt arrived in a package one day, he tried it on and knew immediately that it was, indeed, his.

Somehow, Danny Litwhiler's name is mentioned. Matt and Arleene are good friends of the Litwhilers, who are living in Florida and Arleene speaks up. "You know, Danny had quite a career in baseball. He coached the Florida State University team for many years after he retired from professional baseball. He once played 150 consecutive games without making an error and the glove he used is in the Hall of Fame. He also invented the radar gun that is used to measure the velocity of pitches. The original radar gun is also displayed in the Hall of Fame, but Danny, of course, is not in the Hall of Fame. He likes to say that he is the only player who has a glove and a radar gun in the Hall of Fame, but he's not in it."

"Show Jack all your stuff in the back room," Arleene says, leading us back toward the bedrooms. "The room's a bit of a mess, but you won't mind," she says to me. "We're storing some clothes and things for our daughter while they're building a new house." The walls of the room contain all sorts of framed baseball photographs from Matt's playing days, as well as a few cartoon-like sketches relating highlights of Matt's accomplishments. They are originals of pieces that were published in the newspapers, similar to those done by the famous artist, Willard Mullin, in New

York. At my request, Arleene takes a picture of Matt and me standing in front of some of the photos.

Knowing that Matt and Arleene will be coming to Dallas sometime in the spring to have some surgery on Matt's back, I ask them to consider coming up a day early to see my collection and, if possible, for Matt to be my guest at a game of golf. (He claims to play about 4 times a week.) I give them a business card with my home address and phone number after loading my car for the trip home.

BOBBY BROWN
Ft. Worth, TX
February, 2004

Arriving on time for my meeting at Bobby's home in an established, upper class neighborhood on the west side of Ft. Worth, I am met at the door by Bobby, who invites me to take a seat on the sofa in the living room. Bobby is dressed casually in slacks and is wearing a navy blue sweater over his sport shirt. He appears in good physical shape and displays a pleasant, but direct, no-nonsense manner. The living room is a large room, with bookcases on either side of a fireplace, which is centered on one wall. The bookcases are nicely arranged with a mixture of books (mostly political, military, and social history, with some fiction), family and social photos (including a recent photo of Bobby and his wife with President George Bush and Laura Bush), a few autographed baseballs, and two baseball awards (The Branch Rickey Award for Exceptional Contribution to Baseball, dated 1992, and The Hank Greenberg Hall of Fame Award, presented by the Jewish League of Detroit in 1994). On the wall to the right of where I am seated are two action photographs, one taken at Yankee Stadium, the other at Ebbets Field. Recalling that he had mixed his ballplaying with medical studies, and had eventually served a term a president of the American

League, I opened the conversation by asking him how he managed all the different activities.

"When the war ended in August of 1945, I was a sophomore pre-med student at Tulane. In 1946, with players returning from the war, professional baseball was beginning to get cranked up again and teams were getting aggressive about signing new players. Some offers were made to me, but, initially, I wasn't going to give up my studies to play ball. Finally, the money got too attractive to pass up, so I joined the Yankees. I played baseball from mid-April until mid-October, then went to school for the next 5 months, until baseball season started again. I usually missed most of spring training, but I worked out with some of the good players and teams in the New Orleans area, to keep my skills and timing sharpened. I retired at 29, completed my medical training and residency and was a practicing cardiologist for 25 years here in Ft. Worth. In the mid-80s, when I turned 60, I was asked to interview for the job as commissioner of major league baseball. Bowie Kuhn had just stepped down and they were looking for a replacement. I had a couple of interviews for the job and was eventually told that they really wanted a professional businessman for the job, which I understood. They settled on Peter Ueberroth, but, at about the same time, I got a call from Lee McPhail saying that he was retiring as president of the American League and asking if I was interested in taking the job. I had worked very hard at my cardiology practice and knew I couldn't continue the pace for another 5 years, so, figuring going back to baseball was a lot better than selling suits, I took the job and enjoyed it very much," Bobby explains.

Signing next to his photo in my copy of The Summer of '49, Bobby points to the action photo of Jerry Coleman immediately below his own photo and remarks, "Jerry Coleman...he was the best fielding second baseman I ever saw." High tribute from someone who has seen a lot of second basemen play the game.

After signing the items I have brought, Bobby walks over to the two photos on the wall to the right. "Let me show you these photos," he says. "This one was taken from the roof, behind home plate, at Ebbets Field during the fourth game of the 1949 World Series. I hit a triple with the bases loaded and this photo shows me on the way to first base. Now, look at this," he says, pointing to each figure as he speaks. "Here's Campanella, a Hall of Famer. Here's Hodges, who will probably be a Hall of Famer someday. Here's DiMaggio (running between first and second base), a Hall of Famer. This is Jackie Robinson, a Hall of Famer. Here's Yogi Berra (running between second and third base), a Hall of Famer. Here's 'PeeWee' Reese, a Hall of Famer, and that's Duke Snider, a Hall of Famer. And this is the pitcher, Joe Hatten, who was a teammate of mine at one time." The Yankees won the game 6-4 and Brown led the Yankees in RBIs for the series, with 5.

"How did you like playing in Ebbets Field?" I ask. "I never got to go to a game there."

"Well, that right field wall was fun," he observes. "The fans there were pretty vocal and exuberant and they didn't much care for the Yankees," he adds.

"'Exuberant,'…that's a polite choice of words," I laughingly respond.

Moving to the second picture, Bobby explains, "This picture in Yankee Stadium shows me hitting a pinch-hit double, to tie the score, in the fourth inning of the seventh game of the 1947 World Series. Look at the crowd" The photo clearly shows a completely packed stadium. The accompanying newspaper caption describes the scene in more detail, noting

Billy Johnson scoring from third base and Phil Rizzuto racing from first to third, from where he would eventually score the go-ahead run in the Yankees 5-2 win. The clipping also notes that, with this hit, Bobby Brown established a new World Series record by hitting two doubles, a single, and drawing a base-on-balls in his four plate appearances as a pinch-hitter in the series.

I want to talk more about the 1947 and 1949 World Series, particularly about Joe Page and Hugh Casey, but, not wanting to overstay my welcome, I thank Bobby for his time, gather my things, and prepare to leave. As we walk to the front door, Bobby, knowing that I have recently visited with Mel Parnell, inquires about his health. I give him an update and he seems pleased with my report. "He looks good and he's a really nice guy," I conclude.

"Yes, he is. And he was one helluva' pitcher," Bobby says.

"PREACHER" ROE
West Plains, MO
February, 2004

Preacher had suggested that we meet at the West Plains Municipal Golf Course, where he would be finishing his regular golf game at 3:30, but the weather was cold and windy, so I went directly to his home, where he seemed to be expecting me. The garage door is open as I park in the driveway and Preacher walks out the back door to greet me.

"How're you doin'? I see you didn't have any trouble finding me. Why don't you bring your stuff inside? I'm a bachelor these days. My wife died 2 years ago," he says in his casual southern voice. "Can I help you carry anything?"

He leads me through the kitchen and dining room into the living room, where he turns on a lamp and adjusts the window blinds to provide appropriate light in the room, then suggests I sit in an easy chair. He sits across the room in another chair. At 88, Preacher is alert, displays good mobility, and clearly enjoys company. I ask him about his golf game.

"Oh, we have a little group that plays all the time. Nine holes. Nothin' serious. No cussin' or club throwin', or anything like that. Just a little outdoor fun. I've only been playin' 11 years. Took the game up when I was 77. It kinda' helped me deal with my wife's illness (Alzheimer's). We were married 63 years," he recalls.

"Tell me about the trade that sent you from Pittsburgh to Brooklyn," I say.

"Well, I first came to the big leagues in the Cardinals organization," he begins. "Mr. Rickey ran the organization then, so I was one of his players. Then he left to take over the Brooklyn club and I wound up over in Pittsburgh. I was doing okay there until 1946, when I had a very serious brain and head injury, as the result of a fight at a basketball game in the off season. My head hit the floor, fractured my skull, and lacerated my brain. I was unconscious for 57 hours. I didn't do too well in '47 at Pittsburgh, but, for some reason, Mr. Rickey was still interested in me and paid to have me go up to the Mayo Clinic for evaluation and treatment. When they were ready to send me home, they gave me this rehabilitation regimen that I was supposed to follow. Well, Mr. Rickey sent his brother down to live with me through the winter to see that I was doing what I was supposed to and to report to him whether or not he felt I might be able to help out in Brooklyn. When he said he thought I was worth a try, Mr. Rickey made the trade with Pittsburgh that took me to

Brooklyn with Billy Cox and Gene Mauch for Vic Lombardi, Hal Gregg, and Dixie Walker."

Preacher continues, "At the start of 1948, Mr. Rickey had decided to reconstruct his infield. Gil Hodges was a catcher who could hit, but Campanella was going to do the catching. Robinson was a middle infielder, but he had played at first base in '47. Rickey decided he wanted to make Hodges a first baseman and move Robinson to second base, his natural position. Billy Cox had played shortstop at Pittsburgh, but PeeWee was set at short in Brooklyn, so they made Cox into a third baseman. The press thought the Brooklyn management had lost its mind, changing basically the entire infield of a team that had won the pennant the prior year, but the new infield became one of the best in baseball and remained in place for many years. Mr. Rickey knew what he was doing!

"The Dodgers trained in the Dominican Republic in the spring of 1948 because Jackie Robinson and some other blacks were on the team. That hot weather down there was just what I needed. I always pitched well in hot weather and I had a good spring. When the season got started and the rosters had to be cut, Leo (Durocher) called me and another young left-handed pitcher named Dwain Sloat into his office before a series in Cincinnati. Leo said, 'Look, I'm only going to carry two lefthanders on my pitching staff. Joe Hatten has been here and proven himself for 4 years, so he's got one spot. That leaves the other spot for one of you. I'm going to give you both a shot and I'll keep the one who does the best job. We'll draw cards and whoever picks the high card will pitch tonight and the other will pitch tomorrow.' Well, I drew the high card and pitched a shutout. The next day Sloat pitched a very good game, but lost 2-1, both runs scoring on an error by Reese. So, we go on to Chicago and Leo calls another meeting and says, 'I can't send Sloat down when the only reason he lost is because the 'captain' (Reese) kicked one. We'll do it again.' This time I pulled the high card again and pitched another shutout. Next day, Sloat goes out and is doing fine until about the fifth inning when (Andy) Pafko hits a homer and he gives up 5 runs! So, I get the job and went 12-8 that year."

"Why do you think Rickey liked you so much?" I ask.

"Oh, I don't know. He'd brought me up in St. Louis. When I asked him why he was so interested in having me over in Brooklyn he said, 'Well Preach, you've had so much bad luck I figured you were due for some good luck and I wanted it to be with me.'"

"Preach, you always pitched well against Cincinnati when I was growing up," I comment.

He chuckles and says, "That's a funny thing. You know, Cincinnati looked at me when I was coming up. (Bill) McKechnie was managing the Reds and he came up to watch me pitch a game in Columbus (Ohio). I was pitching against one of the Yankee farm teams and it must have been 106 degrees that day. Really hot! I was pretty skinny. Weighed about 160 pounds. I pitched 12 innings in that heat and won the game, but McKechnie said he didn't think I had enough endurance to pitch in the big leagues. When I got there, I always had good success against Cincinnati and every time I beat them McKechnie would just salute me after the game, like saying 'my mistake.'"

He continues, "I remember pitching a game against Cincinnati in Pittsburgh. I was pitching against Bucky Walters and we both had no-hitters going into the ninth inning. Walters had been a third baseman at one time and was a good hitter. Anyway, he led off the top of the ninth and hit the first pitch I threw for a home run. Frankie Frisch was our manager and he just exploded! Couldn't believe I had given up a home run to the pitcher! He took me out of the game right there! Didn't have anyone warming up or anything. Whoever replaced me gave up another 3 or 4 runs before the inning was over. We got a hit or two in the last of the ninth, but lost the game. Frisch wasn't a bad manager, but I never cared for him after he did that to me."

"Then there was a game I pitched against Ewell Blackwell in Brooklyn. There was no score after about 5 or 6 innings and (Brooklyn manager) Dressen came up to me and said, 'Preach, it looks like Blackie is going to be pretty tough tonight. Just keep us in this thing and I'll think of something.' So we go into the bottom of the ninth in a scoreless tie and Campanella hits a home run to win the game. Everyone's jumping all over Campy and Dressen is jumping all over me yelling, 'See, I told you I'd think of something!'"

Preacher changes the subject. "You know, my biggest disappointment in baseball is that I never got a World Series ring," he opines.

"And you just missed it by one year. You retired in 1954, didn't you?" I note.

"Yes, but I actually tried to retire in 1953. I told Mr. O'Malley I wanted to retire, but he wanted me to stay another year to help develop a new young pitcher he had (Koufax). So, I worked with him on a curveball and pitched a game now and then when they needed a filler," Preacher explains.

As he finishes signing the items I have, Preacher says, "Do you remember a guy named Danny Litwhiler?"

"Sure. He played the outfield for Boston and Cincinnati," I respond.

"That guy used to wear me out. I just couldn't get him out. He hit me like he owned me," Preacher says. "It wasn't until I got to Brooklyn that I started getting him out. We had a pre-game meeting to go over the hitters and how I was going to pitch to them. When we got to Litwhiler, I said, 'If anybody has any ideas, speak up, because nothing I do seems to work.' PeeWee (Reese) asks me what pitch he hits and where he hits it. I tell him that he hits anything I throw up there between short and third. So, PeeWee says, 'Okay, just pitch him the way you always do and I'll take care of it.' When Litwhiler comes up, PeeWee just shades a little toward third base and everything Litwhiler hits, PeeWee comes up with. After that, I had pretty good luck with Litwhiler," Preacher says, smiling.

As I gather my stuff to leave, Preacher says, "I've really enjoyed talking with you. If you have anything else you want me to sign, just send it up to me." He walks with me out to the car and, declining my offer to buy him dinner, says, "No thanks. I'd like to, but I have to stick to a strict diet and I have everything right here."

CHUCK DIERING
St. Louis, MO
February, 2004

A short time after I ring the bell at the front door, I hear the garage door open and Chuck appears, asking, "Can I help you?"

Chuck's phone number is unlisted, so he is not anticipating my visit. I quickly introduce myself and explain the purpose of my visit. He immediately welcomes me and invites me to gather my items from the car and bring them in the house, where we sit at the breakfast room table. The first item he sees is a New York Giants bat, which gets the conversation started.

"Well, I only spent one year (1952) in New York and, as far as I'm concerned, that was sort of a lost year. For whatever reason, Durocher didn't have much use for me and I didn't get much playing time there. My batting average took a beating because I played so irregularly. Willie Mays was Durocher's little pet; couldn't do anything wrong," Chuck observes. "I wasn't a great hitter. I was a damned good outfielder, though. In 1949, with the Cardinals, I played center field. I had Musial on one side, in right field, and Slaughter on the other side, in left field. I handled anything I could get to. That was a very tough luck season for us. We lost the pennant by one game and I remember two games we lost late in the season that we should have won. The first was in Pittsburgh. We had a 2 or 3 run lead in the ninth inning and Tom Saffell hit a grand slam home run to beat us. In another game, we're down by a run and 'Nippy' Jones hits what everyone thinks is a home run with a man on base to win the game. Only 'Jocko' Conlon, the third base umpire has his hands up in the air. He had called a balk on the pitcher, negating the home run, so we lost the game," Chuck declares, shaking his head.

Chuck finishes signing my items and leads me back to his office to show me his memorabilia. Among the photos on the wall, he points to a large team photo of the 1954 Baltimore Orioles. It is autographed by every player except two. Chuck says, "That was the first year for the Orioles and it was my last year in baseball. I didn't know it until just a few years ago, but I held the Orioles' record for the most assists by an outfielder for 35 years! Not bad, eh?"

Chuck takes me downstairs into the basement, where there are more photos from his playing days, as well as an incredible collection of all sorts of things. There are cast models of automobiles and racing cars, an extensive stamp collection, autographed baseball bats, golf balls, golf bag tags, and several large wooden doll houses that Chuck builds as a hobby. He also takes me to a garage behind his house, where he houses 5 classic Ford convertibles, including an original 1954 Thunderbird, along with two other T-birds and two vintage 1950s Ford Mustangs, one a robin's egg blue 1958 model, which he still drives occasionally. He says he plans to divest himself of the cars to his children on Father's Day.

I'm happy to have Chuck's autograph, but the highlight of this visit has definitely been seeing the vast assortment of collectibles that Chuck has accumulated.

JACK BANTA
Hutchinson, KS
February, 2004

A light blue shingle hangs from the corner of the garage, at the beginning of the walkway to the front door of a modest single story home on a large lot in rural Hutchinson. It reads: The Bantas. There are golf motif items in evidence throughout the property. A smiling Jack Banta answers the door, welcomes me inside, and suggests we sit in his computer room. He is tall and husky, slightly stoop shouldered, and his rosy cheeked face resembles his image on the 1950 Bowman baseball card reprint in my collection.

Unknown to some, the highlight of Jack Banta's major league career was his performance as the winning pitcher in Brooklyn's 10 inning victory over Philadelphia in the final game of the 1949 season, which gave the Dodgers the National League pennant by a single game over St. Louis. Daryl Spencer had advised me that that a group was interested in inducting Banta into the Kansas Sports Hall of

Fame, but had been unable to obtain his assent. I asked him about the honor.

"Oh, someone called me about that but I don't know. I really didn't do much. I just had that one good game at the end of the year. My career didn't last long after that, although I did pitch in 3 games of the '49 World Series." Jack seems to be a very modest person and it appears that he is questioning his worthiness to be so honored. He has also had to contend with some serious health issues in the past year and, perhaps, this has occupied his attention. He says that he hopes to be able to start playing some golf later in the year, having had to forego the game because of his health for the past year or so.

I try to encourage him to reconsider his thoughts about the Hall of fame induction. "Well, Jack, just think of all the guys who would have given anything to play in the major leagues at all, not to mention a World Series." Pointing to the pictures of his children and grandchildren displayed on the walls and bookcase in the room, I add, "I'll bet your children and grandchildren would be thrilled to death to have you in that Hall of Fame."

He shrugs and changes the subject to player salaries in his playing days. "When I signed to play in the Pony League in 1944, my salary was $100 a month. Of course, we got meal money when we traveled. When I was promoted to Montreal, which at that time was a double A farm team, my salary was increased to $200 a month. In 1949 with the Dodgers, my salary was $6,000 and my World Series share was an additional $3,000. Quite a bit different from what today's players make."

He also talks about the arm injury that terminated his career. "It was amazing what happened. All of a sudden I just couldn't pitch. I guess it was something like one of those rotator cuff injuries. Today, it could probably be treated or fixed, but in my day we didn't have the medical resources to do anything about it. So, my career ended about as fast as it started."

DARYL SPENCER
Wichita, KS
February, 2004

Daryl has agreed to meet at a Spangles restaurant in downtown Wichita. Arriving early, I find a booth on the sunny side of the restaurant, position a bright orange New York Giants book on the table, where it can be easily seen, and begin reading USA Today. A short while later, Daryl approaches the table and says, "You look like you might be a baseball collector."

He is tall, casually dressed in jeans, sport shirt, and is wearing a navy blue winter jacket. Smiling, he shakes my hand and slides into the seat across the table from me. I mention having watched him play with the Giants when they came to Cincinnati when I was growing up.

Daryl begins, "Cincinnati…I spent some time there. You know, players often have a preference for uniform numbers. I had always worn number 20. When I reported to Cincinnati and walked into the clubhouse for the first time, Frank Robinson, who wore number 20 his entire career, came over to me and asked if I would like to have his uniform number. I thought that was real classy, but, of course, I declined. The other thing was that (Fred) Hutchinson wanted me to room with a rookie infielder he had. I was a pretty 'laid back' kind of guy and Hutch said he wanted me to serve as sort of a calming influence on his hyper-kinetic rookie. The rookie was Pete Rose and he was one bundle of energy. As I said, I was pretty laid back and liked to sleep-in in the mornings. Pete would wake up early in the morning and start doing exercises. You know, jumping jacks and that sort of stuff. He was something else. I couldn't believe it."

"What do you think about Pete and the Hall of Fame?" I ask.

"Jeez, that's tough," Daryl responds. "Pete's done some pretty stupid things in the way he's handled everything. I certainly don't think he should be allowed to come back into professional baseball."

"I agree with that, but how does the game of baseball categorically ignore what he accomplished as a player? I say keep him out of baseball, but recognize his accomplishments as a player in the Hall. His plaque could state that he was subsequently banned from the game for life, but to pretend that the guy never existed is ridiculous," I argue.

"That's sort of how I feel," Daryl concedes.

The conversation turns to managers and Daryl says, "I never really got along with Walt Alston. He was a different sort of guy. I don't think he ever got over my criticizing his handling of the final playoff game with the Giants in 1962. I was on the Dodger club and we were winning that game until the ninth inning. Roebuck had been pitching well in relief, so when he came to bat in the bottom of the eighth, Alston let him bat rather than pinch-hitting for him. Then he takes Gilliam out of the game and puts Larry Burright in at second, as a defensive replacement. Burright was probably a better fielder than Gilliam at that point in his career, but Gilliam was very smart and knew how to play hitters. The Giants had a man on and, I think, one out. Harvey Kuenn, one of the best right field hitters in the game was at bat, so Alston moved Burright a couple of steps toward first base. The way Roebuck was pitching, there was no way Kuenn was going to be able to hit to right. Sure enough, he grounds to Wills at short, who flips to Burright, who had to cover those extra steps from where Alston had moved him, and the throw to first is late. A double play and the game is over, but the Giants then scored four runs and we lose the game and the pennant. If Gilliam had been in the game and Alston had moved him, Jim would have adjusted toward second before the pitch was thrown. Anyway, in the clubhouse after the game, I yelled , 'Who moved Burright?' That was the end of my days as a Dodger."

Daryl continues, "The next year I was at Cincinnati and we were playing the Dodgers. Joey Jay was pitching for us against Koufax and we were down a run or tied late in the game. Vada Pinson doubles to open the inning. Now, Frank Robinson is the hitter and I'm on deck to hit after Robinson. Alston comes out of the dugout and looks at me as he walks to the mound. I know he wants to walk Robinson and pitch to me and he looks over at me again as he walks back to the dugout. Sure enough, they walk Frank. Now, I don't care about beating LA so much as I just want to beat Alston. I knew Koufax well enough to know that the only pitch I might be able to hit hard was a low outside fastball. His fastball tended to rise and his curve broke sharply. Anyway, he gets two strikes on me and then…here it comes…a low fastball on the outside corner. I hit it into the seats. It was one of the happiest moments of my career."

"What's your most memorable experience as a ballplayer?" I ask.

"Well, you'd have to understand my life growing up. My dad loved baseball and he talked about my becoming a ballplayer all the years I was growing up. He died when I was a sophomore in high school. I didn't make the baseball team as a sophomore and I broke my arm and couldn't play as a junior. Somehow, I managed to make it to the big leagues and I'll never forget the day I reported to the Giants at the Polo Grounds. I was with four or five other guys who had been called up and when we entered the gate out in right-centerfield, I just looked up at the outside of the stadium and started to cry. I was thinking of my dad and what it would have meant to him. Emotionally, that was my most memorable experience," Daryl explains.

Daryl claims he was always an early season hitter. "I don't know why, but as long as it was cool and I was wearing a long-sleeved turtleneck undershirt, I hit real well. I was always among the leading hitters in the early part of the season, but when it started getting hot, my average usually dropped considerably. I also went through a period in 1962-63 when, for whatever reason, I hit well on Saturdays nights. I think at one time I had the game winning hit on five consecutive Saturday nights! Also, for some reason, I generally had more trouble hitting left-handed pitching than I did right-handers. Spahn was particularly tough, because he threw sort of a screwball that broke away from right-handed hitters. Musial used to wear him out, but Stan, of course, was left-handed. I just hit right-handers much better than lefties, although a few righties, like Erskine, with that overhand curveball, were tough."

Our business completed, I buy Daryl's lunch and he tells me a little about his baseball experiences in Japan. I thank him for meeting with me and begin my trip home.

FRANK SULLIVAN
Lihue, Kauai, HI
May, 2004

Frank Sullivan is the only person written about in this book that I have not met personally. The circumstances related to that fact are, however, interesting in themselves and I want to share them.

It was almost by accident that I discovered that a former ballplayer, Frank Sullivan, was living in Kauai, where my wife and I were planning to vacation for a week. I picked up the phone, called Frank, introduced myself, and explained that I would like to meet him and obtain his autograph while we were in Kauai. He was quite agreeable to my request and suggested that I just give him another call after we had arrived to set up a meeting. I confirmed the plan in a follow-up note to him. A day or so after arriving in Kauai I called Frank to arrange a meeting. His response was a friendly one. "Sure," he said, "I just had a cataract removed from one of my eyes this morning and I'm supposed to go back to the doctor tomorrow. Why don't we meet Friday? I have a golf game at 7:30, but you can call me around noon and we'll decide where to meet."

Having a golf engagement Friday morning myself, this plan worked out well. Friday, after completing my golf game at Kauai Lagoons, a course I learned Frank Sullivan had helped build and manage for several years, I called the Sullivan house to set up our meeting time and place.

Frank's wife answered the phone and she was obviously somewhat distressed. "Oh, I'm so sorry but Frank has developed a serious infection in his eye and he has to fly to Honolulu right away and have surgery on it this afternoon," she explained. I expressed my concern over the situation, told her that I understood, and asked if I could stay in touch with them to find out how the situation developed. She was quite agreeable.

Several days later, I called the Sullivans from another island to check on Frank's condition. Mrs. Sullivan filled me in. "Well, we got back home today. They cleaned a lot of junk out of his eye, but he can't see anything with it and is just going to have to wait and see if things improve."

A week or so later I contacted Frank by e-mail and he reported that he had not regained his vision from the eye and seemed doubtful that the situation would get much better. Since then we have maintained regular contact by e-mail and have become "pen pals" of a sort. When he learned I was writing a book about my visits with players, he mentioned that he had written many one-page stories about many of his life experiences, both in and out of baseball, and asked if I would be interested in reading them. When I told him of my definite interest, he began sending me 3 or 4 stories a day from his collection of Memories via e-mail. Frank's stories go all the way back to his childhood, but also include many interesting stories from his career in baseball and reflect a great sense of humor. I have encouraged him to consider publishing Memories and have agreed not to divulge any of his material, other than to say that he has some great stories about his old Red Sox batterymate, Sam White, as well as another old catcher, Clint Courtney.

I'm hoping that I will have a chance sometime soon to meet Frank, as he has been a most enjoyable and interesting correspondent.

DAVE WILLIAMS
JOE GARAGIOLA
San Francisco, CA
July, 2004

I was fortunate enough to attend the 50th anniversary reunion of the 1954 New York Giants, held in San Francisco, as the guest of Daryl Spencer. The following stories are from the many that were exchanged during that eventful weekend.

During a conversation about Richie Ashburn, Dave Williams recalled the following: "Ashburn was notorious for being able to protect the plate and foul off good pitches. One day when we were playing the Phillies and Sal Maglie was pitching, Sal ran the count full to Ashburn. Ashburn then proceeded to foul off seven or eight consecutive pitches. I didn't usually go to the mound to talk to pitchers, Alvin (Dark) usually handled that, but this time I walked over to Maglie and said, 'Hey, Sal. Why don't you just walk the guy and then pick him off first?'

"Sal went ballistic! 'Just get your ass back there and play second base, you little shit!' he said."

Joe Garagiola enjoyed talking about playing for Leo Durocher, when he was traded from Pittsburgh to the Giants late in the 1954 season.

"The day that I reported to the Giants, I went to the clubhouse, got my uniform, dressed, and reported for the pre-game meeting. Leo didn't bother to introduce me to the team or anything and he never called me by my name. He just referred to me as 'Dago.' Anyway, at the end of the meeting, Leo says, 'You're catching today, 'Dago'. I don't want to get Westrum hurt.' That was my introduction to Leo and the Giants."

Garagiola continues, "We're playing the Pirates and Murry Dickson is pitching. When Dickson's pitching, you don't know where the ball's going to come from and he throws somewhere between sidearm and underhand, so that the ball is usually coming from low to high. Very tough to hit. The first time up, I strike out. The next time up, we've got two runners on and one out. Dickson gets a couple of strikes on me, but now I'm ready. Next pitch, I hammer the ball to the second baseman, who turns the double play ending the inning. When I get back to the dugout to put on my catcher's equipment, Leo walks over and says to me, 'Why didn't you just strike out. It would have prolonged the inning.'"

EPILOGUE

As many of the players I visited pointed out, the game of baseball has changed greatly since the "Golden Era" of the 1950s. Today's players may be bigger and stronger, but they seem to lack the knowledge and ability to properly execute many of the fundamental skills that were required to succeed in earlier times. Certainly, the skills and endurance required of pitchers in earlier times is no longer in evidence. As the world of Major League Baseball grew as a result of television, league expansion, and the incorporation of the designated hitter in the American League, the overall quality of play at every position declined, as players with lesser levels of talent were brought up to fill team rosters. And then, of course, there is the issue of money. Television brought money to the game as it had not seen before. It also brought a much higher degree of awareness on the part of umpires, as well as players, that they were actors on a gigantic stage. The "old ball park" became just another theatre. As players' salaries increased, so did their sense of independence, not only from the owners, but, perhaps more significantly, from the fans and cities they represented, as well as from their own teammates. Roommates became a thing of the past and with them went the "family" feeling that was an integral part of baseball in earlier times. The commitment to teammates and hometown fans has been replaced by commitment to self. The result of these changes, it seems to me, is that the players of today are no longer representative of the general American population in terms of typical work requirements, earning power, and lifestyle. Sadly, I have virtually no interest in Major League Baseball as it is played today, but I cherish my memories of the game and of the players who played it when I was growing up.

There's something special about all of the players I visited, including many who are not included in this book. (Unfortunately, my records of visits with many other players were lost because I failed to "back up" files that were lost as the result of a computer error.) Each of them displayed certain personality traits and social behaviors that, apparently, if not unique to their generation, have, to a significant extent, been lost among most recent time and present day celebrities. The traits and behaviors are the same ones that Tom Brokaw identified in his book, The Greatest Generation, and articulated so eloquently in his address at the dedication ceremonies of the World War II Memorial in Washington, D.C. on Memorial Day of this year. These former players and their wives all displayed a genuine attitude of humility, consideration, graciousness, and hospitality during my visits, even when those visits were unannounced. They all expressed interest in how my hobby was going and appreciation that I was interested in them and their lives since leaving baseball. Several have become personal friends with whom I maintain contact by letter, phone, or e-mail. None displayed the slightest arrogance or self-importance that I have seen so frequently among the more recent generations of ballplayers.

Commitment is another trait that strikes me when I think of these players. The players that I visited, virtually without exception, remain married to their original wives. Divorce simply is not in evidence. Certainly, being the wife of a major league baseball player in the 1940s and 1950s could not have been an easy or glamorous existence. Imagine Larry Jansen's wife raising 10 children! And the commitments continue. Virginia Voiselle, with health problems of her own, continues to care for her husband, Bill, who has suffered several debilitating strokes, and his brother, Jim, a widower who lives down the street. George Strickland continues to care for his Alzheimer's stricken wife at home. Carl and Betty Erskine still care for their Down syndrome stricken son, Jimmy, now 44 years old and still living with them at home. These are just a few examples of the same type of commitments these players made to teammates, owners, and fans during their playing careers.

Consideration and generosity are also traits I saw time and again. If you re-read the stories in this book, take note of the number of times a player or his wife was dealing with illness and yet would not decline my visit, in spite of my own suggestion that the visit be postponed. I was amazed at the number of times such situations presented themselves and how consistently the players responded in such a selfless and gracious way. It causes me to re-think how I respond to others at times of inconvenience or interruption and helps remind me that it's people that are important. Other people, not one's self.

My hobby continues to be a wonderful and exciting experience. It keeps alive wonderful memories of my youth, when the game of baseball is what I lived for and my parents and grandparents encouraged my interest in it. It reminds me of the many thrills and disappointments I experienced as an amateur ballplayer and, later, as a coach. It helps keep alive a certain respect and appreciation for the past and a realization that not all things improve with time and change.

I'm generally an optimistic and forward thinking person, but I've learned that there are wonderful things to be learned and experienced by maintaining a connection with the past. Thomas Wolfe wrote You Can't Go Home Again, but my experiences visiting with these wonderful people have not only rekindled wonderful memories of the past, but also provided an example to follow as I pursue the future.

PLAYER INDEX